KT-212-154

Withdrawn For Sale

Withdrawn For Sale

animal hats

animal hats

15 KNITTED PROJECTS TO KEEP YOU WARM AND TOASTY

VANESSA MOONCIE

First published 2012 by
Guild of Master Craftsman
Publications Ltd
Castle Place, 166 High Street, Lewes,
East Sussex BN7 1XU

Text and designs © Vanessa Mooncie, 2012
Copyright in the Work © GMC Publications
Ltd, 2012

ISBN 978-1-86108-824-6

All rights reserved

The right of Vanessa Mooncie to be
identified as the author of this work
has been asserted in accordance with
the Copyright, Designs and Patents Act
1988, sections 77 and 78.

No part of this publication may be
reproduced, stored in a retrieval system
or transmitted in any form or by any means
without the prior permission of the publisher
and copyright owner.

This book is sold subject to the condition
that all designs are copyright and are
not for commercial reproduction without
the permission of the designer and
copyright owner.

The publishers and author can accept
no legal responsibility for any consequences
arising from the application of information,
advice or instructions given in this publication.

A catalogue record for this book is available
from the British Library.

Publisher Jonathan Bailey
Production Manager Jim Bulley
Managing Editor Gerrie Purcell
Senior Project Editor Virginia Brehaut
Managing Art Editor Gilda Pacitti
Design Rebecca Mothersole
Photographer Chris Gloag

Set in Neo Sans
Colour origination by GMC Reprographics
Printed and bound in China by Hung Hing
Printing Co. Ltd

contents

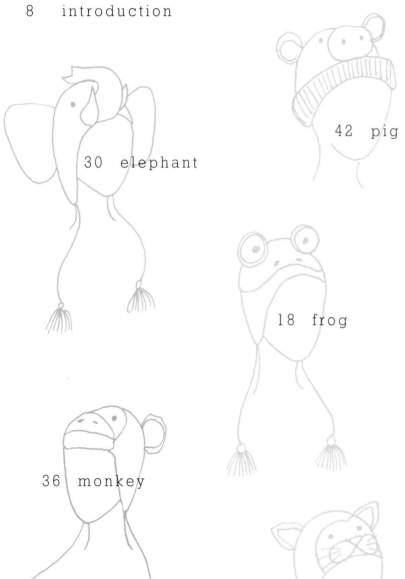

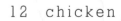

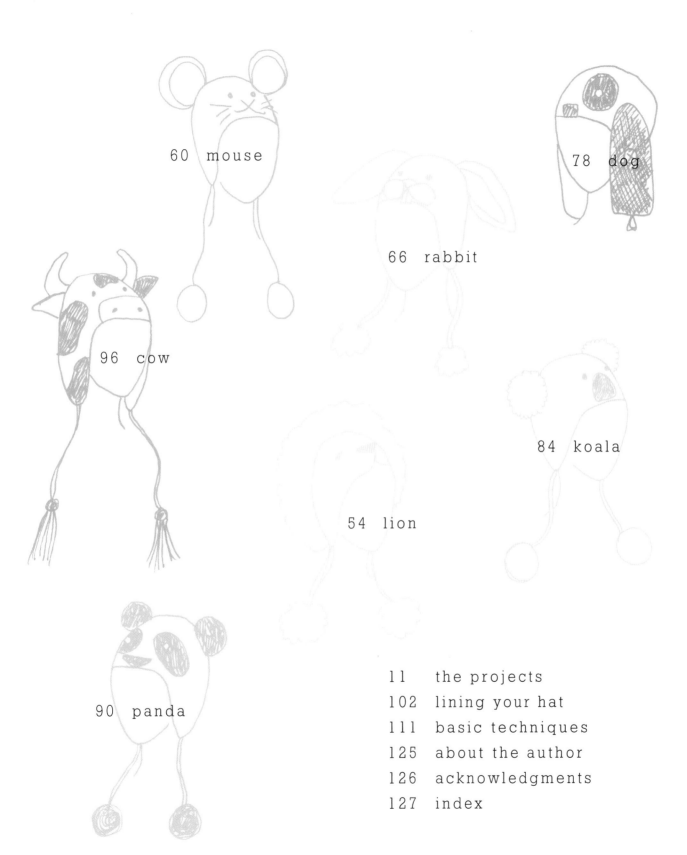

introduction

This book brings together a collection of 15 fun and unique knitted hat designs, which are aimed at both children and grown-ups. Much inspiration was drawn from historical animal apparel, such as Baby Bunting's rabbit skin in the popular nursery rhyme and the ornate animal and bird headdresses that traditionally adorned the heads of Native Americans.

Each hat project is given in a child's and adult's size. As well as giving guidance and tips on starting the projects, there are two options for lining the hats to make them warm and cosy: sewing a soft fleece fabric lining or a snuggly knitted lining.

This book of patterns will help decorate your head and keep you snug with a sense of fun, and is a must-have companion for exuberant headwear and great handcrafted gift ideas.

the projects

chicken

Here is one hen that won't be sitting on a nest
of freshly laid eggs like her feathered friends,
but will perch comfortably on your head, making
you warm and toasty on a chilly day.

MATERIALS

Wendy Merino Chunky, 100% merino wool
(71yds/65m per 50g ball)
3[3] x 50g balls in 2470 Cloud (A)
1[1] x 50g ball in 2475 Poppy (B)
Oddment of Aran yarn in yellow (C)
1 pair each of 7mm (UK2:US10.5/11) and 4.5mm
(UK7:US7) knitting needles
2 x brown ¾[⅞]in (2[2.25]cm) diameter buttons
2 x black ½[⅝]in (1.25[1.5]cm) diameter buttons
Small amount of toy stuffing
Stitch holder
Darning needle
Sewing needle
Black sewing thread
Thin card to make pompoms

SIZES

To fit: child up to 8 years [adult]

TENSION

13 sts and 18 rows to 4in (10cm) over stocking
stitch using 7mm needles. Use larger or smaller
needles if necessary to obtain correct tension.

METHOD

The main section is knitted first. The open beak is worked in two halves then stuffed and stitched together before attaching to the front of the hat. The comb is a simple piece in garter stitch, shaped by decreasing and casting on stitches. The yarn is doubled to create a denser fabric, which helps it to stand up.

MAIN PIECE
First earflap
Both sizes
*Using 7mm needles and A, cast on 3 sts.
Row 1 (inc) (RS): Kfb, k1, kfb (5 sts).
Row 2: K2, p1, k2.
Row 3 (inc): Kfb, k3, kfb (7 sts).
Row 4: K2, p3, k2.
Row 5 (inc): Kfb, k5, kfb (9 sts).
Row 6: K2, p5, k2.
Row 7 (inc): Kfb, k7, kfb (11 sts).
Row 8: K2, p7, k2.
Row 9 (inc): Kfb, k9, kfb (13 sts).
Row 10: K2, p9, k2.
Row 11 (inc): Kfb, k11, kfb (15 sts).
Row 12: K2, p11, k2.
Adult size only
Row 13 (inc): Kfb, k13, kfb (17 sts).
Row 14: K2, p13, k2.
Both sizes
Row 15: Knit.
Row 16: As row 12[14].*
Break yarn and leave these sts on a holder.

Second earflap
Work as given for first earflap from * to *.
Next row: Cast on and k 5 sts, knit across 15[17] sts of second earflap, turn, cast on 21 sts, turn, knit across 15[17] sts of first earflap, turn, cast on 5 sts (61[65] sts).
Next row (WS): K7, p11[13], k25, p11[13], k7.
Next row: Knit.
Rep last 2 rows once more and then starting with a purl row, work 19[21] rows in st st, ending with a WS row.

Shape crown
Row 1 (RS) (dec): K2tog, (k12[13], sl1, k2tog, psso) 3 times, k12[13], k2tog (53[57] sts).
Row 2: Purl.
Row 3 (dec): K2tog, (k10[11], sl1, k2tog, psso) 3 times, k10[11], k2tog (45[49] sts).
Row 4: Purl.
Row 5 (dec): K2tog, (k8[9], sl1, k2tog, psso) 3 times, k8[9], k2tog (37[41] sts).
Row 6: Purl.
Row 7 (dec): K2tog, (k6[7], sl1, k2tog, psso) 3 times, k6[7], k2tog (29[33] sts).
Row 8: Purl.
Row 9 (dec): K2tog, (k4[5], sl1, k2tog, psso) 3 times, k4[5], k2tog (21[25] sts).
Row 10: Purl.
Row 11 (dec): K2tog, (k2[3], sl1, k2tog, psso) 3 times, k2[3], k2tog (13[17] sts).
Adult size only
Row 12: Purl.
Row 13 (dec): K2tog, (k1, sl1, k2tog, psso) 3 times, k1, k2tog (9 sts).
Both sizes
Break yarn and thread through rem sts, draw up tight and fasten off.

EARFLAP FACING (MAKE 2)

Omit if you plan to add knitted lining

Using 7mm needles and A, cast on 3 sts and work rows 1 to 16 of pattern for earflaps.

Next: Rep rows 15 and 16 three more times.

Cast off loosely.

BEAK (MAKE 2)

With 4.5mm needles and C, cast on 15[19] sts.

Adult size only

Row 1 (dec) (RS): K2tog, k6, sl1, k2tog, psso, k6, k2tog (15 sts).

Row 2: Purl.

Both sizes

Row 3 (dec): K2tog, k4, sl1, k2tog, psso, k4, k2tog (11 sts).

Row 4: Purl.

Row 5 (dec): K2tog, k2, sl1, k2tog, psso, k2, k2tog (7 sts).

Row 6: Purl.

Row 7 (dec): K2, sl1, k2tog, psso, k2 (5 sts).

Break yarn and thread through rem sts, draw up and fasten off. Sew the side seam and stuff lightly, keeping a flattened shape. Stitch both sides of the cast-on edge together to close. This makes one half of the beak.

COMB

With 7mm needles and B DOUBLED, cast on 9[11] sts.

Adult size only

Row 1: K7, k2tog, k2 (10 sts).

Row 2: Knit.

Row 3: K6, k2tog, k2 (9 sts).

Row 4: Knit.

Both sizes

Row 5: K5, k2tog, k2 (8 sts).

Row 6: Knit.

Row 7: K4, k2tog, k2 (7 sts).

Row 8: Knit.

Row 9: K3, k2tog, k2 (6 sts).

Row 10: Knit.

Row 11: K2, k2tog, k2 (5 sts).

Row 12: Knit.

Row 13: K1, k2tog, k2 (4 sts).

Row 14: Knit.

Row 15: Cast on and k5[7], k2tog, k2 (8[10] sts).

Rep rows 6[2]–15 then rows 6[2]–13.

Cast off.

MAKING UP

Using matching yarn, join the back seam.

With right sides together, sew the earflap facings to the earflaps, starting and finishing at the edge of the main section, leaving the overlapping cast-on edge open. Turn right side out and slipstitch the open edges to the inside of the main section.

Sew the comb over the centre of the top of the hat from the front to the back.

Join the two halves of the beak by stitching across the cast-off edges. Sew to the centre front of the hat, just above the garter-stitch border.

Make two twisted cords using A (see page 118), each measuring 8[12]in (20[30]cm) long, using 6[8] strands of yarn. Make two 2[2⅜]in (5[6]cm) pompoms in A (see page 118) and attach each to one end of the twisted cord, then stitch the other end of the cord to the tip of the earflap.

Using sewing thread, place the small black buttons over the larger brown buttons and sew in place for the eyes.

LINING THE HAT

See pages 104–109 for how to make and attach a cosy fleece or knitted lining for your hat.

frog

A pair of huge, bulging eyes and super-sized tassels give this amazing amphibian a great sense of fun. The soft, super-chunky yarn makes this cold-blooded creature extra warm and cosy.

MATERIALS

Sirdar Big Softie Super Chunky, 51% wool,
    49% acrylic (49yds/45m per 50g ball)
2[2] x 50g balls in 325 (A)
2[2] x 50g balls in 321 (B)
Oddment of chunky yarn in white (C)
1 pair each of 10mm (UK000:US15) and
    7mm (UK2:US10.5/11) needles
2 x black ¾[⅞]in (2[2.25]cm) diameter buttons
2 x black ½in (1.25cm) diameter buttons
Stitch holder
Darning needle
Sewing needle
Black sewing thread
Small amount of toy stuffing
Thin card to make tassels

SIZES

To fit: child up to 8 years [adult]

TENSION

9 sts and 12 rows to 4in (10cm) over stocking
stitch using 10mm needles. Use larger or smaller
needles if necessary to obtain correct tension.

METHOD

The main section of the hat is knitted first, starting with the earflaps. The face is formed with a simple intarsia pattern in a lighter shade of green worked in garter stitch. The eyes are knitted separately with the whites stuffed to form balls then slipped into knitted sockets, shaped like mini hats. Buttons finish the face and tassels decorate the twisted cords.

MAIN PIECE
First earflap
Both sizes
*With 10mm needles and A, cast on 3 sts.
Row 1 (inc) (RS): Kfb, k1, kfb (5 sts).
Row 2: K2, p1, k2.
Row 3 (inc): Kfb, k3, kfb (7 sts).
Row 4: K2, p3, k2.

Row 5 (inc): Kfb, k5, kfb (9 sts).
Row 6: K2, p5, k2.
Adult size only
Row 7 (inc): Kfb, k7, kfb (11 sts).
Row 8: K2, p7, k2.
Both sizes
Row 9: Knit.
Row 10: As row 6[8].*
Break yarn and leave these sts on a holder.

Second earflap
Work as given for first earflap from * to *.
Next row: Cast on and k 4 sts, knit across 9[11] sts of second earflap, turn, cast on 15 sts, turn, knit across 9[11] sts of first earflap, turn, cast on 4 sts (41[45] sts).
Next row (WS): K6, p5[7], k19, p5[7], k6.
Next row: Knit.
Rep first of last 2 rows once more.
Work following 7 rows of intarsia from chart or as given below:
Row 1 (RS): K6[7]A, k6[7]B, k17A, k6[7]B, k6[7]A.
Row 2: P6[7]A, k6[7]B, p17A, k6[7]B, p6[7]A.
Row 3: K4[5]A, k2B, p6[7]B, k2B, k13A, k2B, p6[7]B, k2B, k4[5]A.
Row 4: P4[5]A, k10[11]B, p13A, k10[11]B, p4[5]A.
Row 5: K2[3]A, k2B, p10[11]B, k2B, k9A, k2B, p10[11]B, k2B, k2[3]A.
Row 6: P2[3]A, k14[15]B, p9A, k14[15]B, p2[3]A.
Row 7: K2[3]A, p14[15]B, k9A, p14[15]B, k2[3]A.
Row 8: K to end in B.
Row 9: P to end in B.

Continue in yarn B.
Rep last 2 rows 3 more times, then row 8 again, to end on WS row.
Shape crown
Row 1 (dec): P2tog, (p7[8], sl1 purl wise, p2tog, psso) 3 times, p7[8], p2tog (33[37] sts).
Row 2: Knit.
Row 3 (dec): P2tog, (p5[6], sl1 purl wise, p2tog, psso) 3 times, p5[6], p2tog (25[29] sts).
Row 4: Knit.
Row 5 (dec): P2tog, (p3[4], sl1 purl wise, p2tog, psso) 3 times, p3[4], p2tog (17[21] sts).
Row 6: Knit.
Row 7 (dec): P2tog, (p1[2], sl1 purl wise, p2tog, psso) 3 times, p1[2], p2tog (9[13] sts).
Break yarn and thread through rem sts, draw up tight and fasten off.

EARFLAP FACING (MAKE 2)
Omit if you plan to add knitted lining
With 10mm needles and A, cast on 3 sts and work rows 1 to 10 of pattern for earflaps.
Next: Rep rows 9 and 10 three more times.
Cast off loosely.

FROG CHART (7 rows x 41[45] sts)

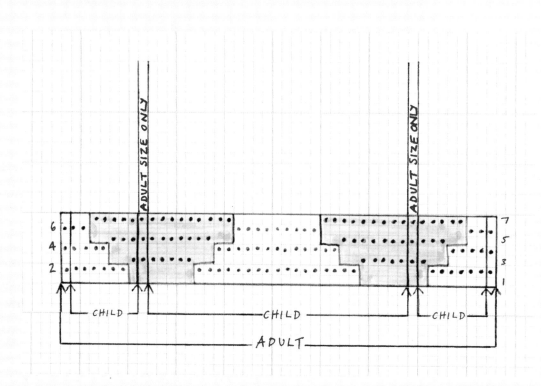

KEY

☐ KNIT
☑ PURL
☐ YARN A
▨ YARN B

EYEBALLS (MAKE 2)

With 7mm needles and C, cast on 9 sts.

Row 1 (inc): (K1, kfb) 4 times, k1 (13 sts).

Adult size only

Row 2: Purl.

Row 3 (inc): (K1, kfb) 6 times, k1 (19 sts).

Both sizes

Starting with a p row, work 5[7] rows in st st.

Adult size only

Row 13 (dec): (K1, k2tog) 6 times, k1 (13 sts).

Row 14: Purl.

Both sizes

Row 15 (dec): (K1, k2tog) 4 times, k1 (9 sts).

Break yarn and thread through remaining sts, draw up to gather and fasten off.

EYE SOCKETS (MAKE 2)

With 10mm needles and A, cast on 17[21] sts.

Starting with a k row, work 3 rows in garter st.

Row 4 (dec) (RS): (K2tog[k1], k1[k2tog]) 5[7] times k2tog[k0] (11[14] sts).

Knit 1[3] rows.

Next row (dec): (K2tog, k1) 3[4] times, k2tog (7[9] sts).

Break yarn, thread through remaining sts, draw up to gather and fasten off.

MAKING UP

Using matching yarn, join the back seam.

With right sides together, sew the earflap facings to the earflaps, starting and finishing at the edge of the main section, leaving the overlapping cast-on edge open. Turn right side out and slipstitch the open edges to the inside of the main section.

With right sides together, sew the back seam of the eyeball. Turn right side out and stuff to form a ball shape before running a gathering st around the cast-on edge to close.

Join the seam of the eye socket. Slip the eyeball inside so the seam is at the back and the gathered ends are hidden inside the socket. Stitch carefully in place. Attach to the main section of the hat so the seam of the socket is facing down.

Make two twisted cords using A (see page 118), each measuring 8[12]in (20[30]cm) long, using 4[6] strands of yarn. Make two tassels (see page 119) measuring 4[5⅛]in (10[13]cm) long in B, and attach each to one end of the twisted cord, then stitch the other end of the cord to the tip of the earflap.

Using sewing thread, sew the large buttons to the middle of the eyeballs and the small buttons in place at the front of the hat for the nostrils.

LINING THE HAT

See pages 104–109 for how to make and attach a cosy fleece or knitted lining for your hat.

penguin

With his woolly wings to warm your ears, this smart,
suited penguin has a bow tie, with a little sparkle. It can
be pinned onto the hat or, alternatively, used to dress
up your own shirt collar.

MATERIALS

Twilleys Freedom Purity Chunky, 85% wool,
    15% alpaca (79yds/72m per 50g ball)
3[3] x 50g balls in 785 Coal (A)
1[1] x 50g ball in 787 Limestone (B)
Rowan Shimmer, 60% cupro, 40% polyester
    (191yds/175m per 25g ball)
1[1] x 25g ball in 095 Jet (C)
Oddment of DK yarn in black (D)
1 pair each of 7mm (UK2:US10.5/11) and
    4mm (UK8:US6) needles
2 x blue or white 7/8in (2.25cm) diameter buttons
2 x black 7/8in (2.25cm) diameter buttons
2 x black 5/8in (1.5cm) diameter buttons
Darning needle
Sewing needle
Black sewing thread
Brooch bar
Small amount of toy stuffing

SIZES

To fit: child up to 8 years [adult]

TENSION

13 sts and 18 rows to 4in (10cm) over stocking
stitch using 7mm needles. Use larger or smaller
needles if necessary to obtain correct tension.

METHOD

The main piece is in a simple intarsia design. The wings and beak are knitted separately, with the buttons added for eyes and to fasten the wings up for an alternative look. A brooch bar allows the bow tie to be pinned where preferred.

WING FACINGS (MAKE 2)

Both sizes

Using 7mm needles and A, cast on 5 sts.
Row 1 (RS) (inc): Kfb, k3, kfb (7 sts).
Row 2: Knit.
Row 3 (inc): Kfb, k5, kfb (9 sts).
Row 4: Knit.
Row 5 (inc): Kfb, k7, kfb (11 sts).
Row 6: Knit.
Row 7 (inc): Kfb, k9, kfb (13 sts).

Adult size only

Row 8: Knit.
Row 9 (inc): Kfb, k11, kfb (15 sts).

Both sizes

Continue without shaping in garter st (k every row) until work measures 4¾[6] in (12[15]cm) from cast-on edge, ending with a WS row. Break yarn and leave these sts on a holder.

MAIN PIECE

The following is worked in intarsia:
Using 7mm needles and A, cast on 8 sts, turn and k across 13[15] sts of one ear facing, turn. Join in B and cast on 19 sts, turn and k across 13[15] sts of other ear facing in A, turn and cast on 8 sts in A (61[65] sts).
Next row: K21[23]A, k19B, k21[23]A.
Rep last row 3 more times.
Next row (WS): P21[23]A, p19B, p21[23]A.
Next row (RS): K21[23]A, k19B, k21[23]A.
Rep last 2 rows 4 times more, then first of the previous 2 rows once again to end with a WS row.

Adult size only

Work 2 more rows.

Both sizes

Work next 8 rows in patt from the chart or as given below:
Row 1: K22[24]A, k7B, k3A, k7B, k22[24]A.
Row 2: P22[24]A, p7B, p3A, p7B, p22[24]A.
Row 3: K22[24]A, k6B, k5A, k6B, k22[24]A.
Row 4: P22[24]A, p6B, p5A, p6B, p22[24]A.
Row 5: K23[25]A, k4B, k7A, k4B, k23[25]A.
Row 6: P23[25]A, p4B, p7A, p4B, p23[25]A.
Row 7: K to end in A.
Row 8: P to end in A.

Shape crown

Row 1 (RS) (dec): K2tog, k11[12], sl1, k2tog, psso, (k13[14], sl1, k2tog, psso) twice, k11[12], k2tog (53[57] sts).
Row 2: Purl.
Row 3 (dec): K2tog, k9[10], sl1, k2tog, psso, (k11[12], sl1, k2tog, psso) twice, k9[10], k2tog (45[49] sts).
Row 4: Purl.
Row 5 (dec): K2tog, k7[8], sl1, k2tog, psso, (k9[10], sl1, k2tog, psso) twice, k7[8], k2tog (37[41] sts).
Row 6: Purl.
Row 7 (dec): K2tog, k5[6], sl1, k2tog, psso, (k7[8], sl1, k2tog, psso) twice, k5[6], k2tog (29[33] sts).
Row 8: Purl.
Row 9 (dec): K2tog, k3[4], sl1, k2tog, psso, (k5[6], sl1, k2tog, psso) twice, k3[4], k2tog (21[25] sts).
Row 10: Purl.
Row 11 (dec): K2tog, k1[2], sl1, k2tog, psso, (k3[4], sl1, k2tog, psso) twice, k1[2], k2tog (13[17] sts).

Adult size only

Row 12: Purl.
Row 13 (dec): K2tog, sl1, k2tog, psso, (k2, sl1, k2tog, psso) twice, k2tog (9 sts).

Both sizes

Break yarn and thread through rem sts, draw up tight and fasten off.

PENGUIN CHART (8 rows x 61[65] sts)

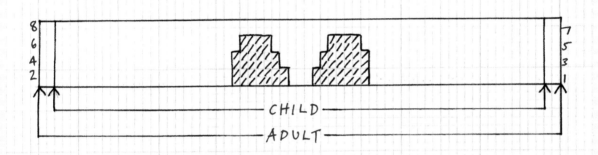

KEY

☐	YARN A
▨	YARN B

WINGS (MAKE 2)
Both sizes
Using 7mm needles and B, cast on 3 sts, (pass previous st over st just made, slipping it off the needle, cast on 1) 3 times to make buttonhole.

Row 1 (WS): K1, turn, cast on 3 sts, turn, k1 (5 sts).

Row 2 (RS) (inc): Kfb, k3, kfb (7 sts).

Row 3: Knit.

Row 4 (inc): Kfb, k5, kfb (9 sts).

Row 5: Knit.

Row 6 (inc): Kfb, k7, kfb (11 sts).

Row 7: Knit.

Row 8 (inc): Kfb, k9, kfb (13 sts).

Adult size only
Row 9: Knit.

Row 10 (inc): Kfb, k11, kfb (15 sts).

Both sizes
Continue in garter st until work measures 7[8¼]in (18[21]cm) from cast-on edge of row 1, ending with a WS row.

Shape top
Next row (dec): K1, k2tog, k to last 3 sts, k2tog, k1.

Next row: Knit.

Rep last 2 rows until 9 sts rem, then rep the first of the last 2 rows once more (7 sts).

Cast off 7 sts.

BEAK
Both sizes
With 4mm needles and C and D worked together, cast on 21 sts.

Row 1 (dec): K2tog, k7, sl1, k2tog, psso, k7, k2tog (17 sts).

Row 2: Purl.

Row 3 (dec): K2tog, k5, sl1, k2tog, psso, k5, k2tog (13 sts).

Row 4: Purl.

Row 5 (dec): K2tog, k3, sl1, k2tog, psso, k3, k2tog (9 sts).

Row 6: Purl.

Row 7 (dec): K2tog, k1, sl1, k2tog, psso, k1, k2tog (5 sts).

Break yarn and thread through rem sts, draw up and fasten off.

BOW TIE
Both sizes
With 7mm needles and A and C worked together, cast on 8 sts.

Work in garter st for 7in (18cm).

Cast off.

KNOT
Both sizes
Cast on 4 sts.

Work 10 rows in garter st.

Cast off.

MAKING UP
Using matching yarn, join the back seam of main section. Position the wrong side of wings over right side of facings and hat. Slipstitch in place, leaving the buttonholes free.

Join the seam of the beak to form a cone and stuff before attaching to the centre front of the hat, just below the point where yarn A meets yarn B, with the seam facing downwards.

Using sewing thread, sew a large black button to each of the tops of the wings. Place the small black buttons over the blue or white buttons and stitch to the main section for the eyes.

Fold the main part of the bow tie in half and join the short edges. Place the seam of the bow tie at the centre back. Take the short piece, which makes up the knot, and wrap it around the centre of the main piece, covering the seam. Join the short edges of the knot and sew in place. This will pull in the middle of the main piece to give the effect of the bow. Sew a brooch bar to the back of the bow tie. Pin to the front of the penguin.

LINING THE HAT
See pages 104–109 for how to make and attach a cosy fleece or knitted lining for your hat.

elephant

Whilst elephants' ears keep them cool, this hat will
keep the wearer warm and protected from the elements.
The tweed yarn with flecks of bright hues running
through it gives tiny touches of colour.

MATERIALS

Sublime Chunky Merino Tweed, 80% wool, 10%
viscose, 10% acrylic (87yds/80m per 50g ball)
4[4] x 50g balls in 235 Pigeon (A)
Sublime Extra Fine Merino Wool DK, 100% merino
wool (127yds/116m per 50g ball)
1[1] x 50g balls in 003 Alabaster (B)
1 pair each of 7mm (UK2:US10.5/11)
and 4mm (UK8:US6) needles
2 x white ¾[⅞]in (2[2.25]cm) diameter buttons
2 x black ½[⅝]in (1.25[1.5]cm) diameter buttons
Small amount of toy stuffing
Stitch holder
Darning needle
Sewing needle
Black sewing thread
Thin card to make tassels

SIZES

To fit: child up to 8 years [adult]

TENSION

13 sts and 18 rows to 4in (10cm) over stocking
stitch using 7mm needles. Use larger or smaller
needles if necessary to obtain correct tension.

METHOD

The hat is knitted in stocking stitch, starting with the triangular earflaps. The ears are in garter stitch, lightly stuffed and stitched to the main part. The trunk and tusks are worked with the yarn doubled to create a firmer fabric. The elephant is finished with button eyes and tassels hanging from twisted cords.

MAIN PIECE

First earflap

Both sizes

*Using 7mm needles and A, cast on 3 sts.

Row 1 (inc) (RS): Kfb, k1, kfb (5 sts).

Row 2: K2, p1, k2.

Row 3 (inc): Kfb, k3, kfb (7 sts).

Row 4: K2, p3, k2.

Row 5 (inc): Kfb, k5, kfb (9 sts).

Row 6: K2, p5, k2.

Row 7 (inc): Kfb, k7, kfb (11 sts).

Row 8: K2, p7, k2.

Row 9 (inc): Kfb, k9, kfb (13 sts).

Row 10: K2, p9, k2.

Row 11 (inc): Kfb, k11, kfb (15 sts).

Row 12: K2, p11, k2.

Adult size only

Row 13 (inc): Kfb, k13, kfb (17 sts).

Row 14: K2, p13, k2.

Both sizes

Row 15: Knit.

Row 16: As row 12[14].*

Break yarn and leave these sts on a holder.

Second earflap

Work as given for first earflap from * to *.

Next row: Cast on and k 5 sts, knit across 15[17] sts of second earflap, turn, cast on 21 sts, turn, knit across 15[17] sts of first earflap, turn, cast on 5 sts (61[65] sts).

Next row (WS): K7, p11[13], k25, p11[13], k7.

Next row: Knit.

Rep last 2 rows once more and then, starting with a purl row, work 19[21] rows in st st, ending with a WS row.

Shape crown

Row 1 (RS) (dec): K2tog, (k12[13], sl1, k2tog, psso) 3 times, k12[13], k2tog (53[57] sts).

Row 2: Purl.

Row 3 (dec): K2tog, (k10[11], sl1, k2tog, psso) 3 times, k10[11], k2tog (45[49] sts).

Row 4: Purl.

Row 5 (dec): K2tog, (k8[9], sl1, k2tog, psso) 3 times, k8[9], k2tog (37[41] sts).

Row 6: Purl.

Row 7 (dec): K2tog, (k6[7], sl1, k2tog, psso) 3 times, k6[7], k2tog (29[33] sts).

Row 8: Purl.

Row 9 (dec): K2tog, (k4[5], sl1, k2tog, psso) 3 times, k4[5], k2tog (21[25] sts).

Row 10: Purl.

Row 11 (dec): K2tog, (k2[3], sl1, k2tog, psso) 3 times, k2[3], k2tog (13[17] sts).

Adult size only

Row 12: Purl.

Row 13 (dec): K2tog, (k1, sl1, k2tog, psso) 3 times, k1, k2tog (9 sts).

Both sizes

Break yarn and thread through rem sts, draw up tight and fasten off.

EARFLAP FACING (MAKE 2)

Omit if you plan to add knitted lining

Using 7mm needles and A, cast on 3 sts and work as for earflaps.

Next: Rep rows 15 and 16 three more times. Cast off loosely.

OUTER EAR (MAKE 2)

With 7mm needles and A, cast on 12[14] sts.

Rows 1-2: Knit.

Row 3 (inc): Kfb, k to last st, kfb (14[16] sts).

Row 4 (inc): Kfb, k to end (15[17] sts).

Rep last 2 rows until there are 21[23] sts.

Next row (inc): K to last st, kfb (22[24] sts).

Next row (inc): Kfb, k to end (23[25] sts).

K1[3] rows without shaping.

Next row (dec): K2tog, k to end (22[24] sts).

Next row (dec): K to last 2 sts, k2tog (21[23] sts).

Rep last 2 rows once more (19[21] sts).

Next row (dec): K2tog, k to end (18[20] sts).

Next row (dec): K2tog, k to last 2 sts, k2tog (16[18] sts).

Next row (dec): K2tog, k to end (15[17] sts).

Rep last 2 rows twice more (9[11] sts).

Next row (dec): K2tog, k to last 2 sts, k2tog (7[9]sts).

Adult size only

Next row (dec): K2tog, k to last 2 sts, k2tog (7 sts).

Both sizes

Cast off.

INNER EAR (MAKE 2)
Work as given for outer ear.

TRUNK
With 7mm needles and A DOUBLED, cast on 19[21] sts.
Row 1 (dec): K2tog, k to last 2 sts, k2tog (17[19] sts).
Row 2: Purl.
Row 3: Kfb, k6[7], sl1, k2tog, psso, k6[7], kfb.
Row 4: Purl.
Rep last 2 rows twice more.
Row 9: As row 3.
Row 10: Kfb, p6[7], p2tog, slip the stitch just worked onto the left-hand needle and pass the next st over it, slip the stitch back onto the right-hand needle, p6[7], kfb.
Rep last 2 rows 5 more times.
Row 21 (dec): K7[8], sl1, k2tog, psso, k7[8] (15[17] sts).
Row 22: Purl.
Adult size only
Row 23 (dec): K7, sl1, k2tog, psso, k7 (15 sts).
Row 24: Purl.
Shape top
Both sizes
Next row: Cast off 4 sts, k to end (11 sts).
Next row: Cast off 4 sts, p to end (7 sts).
Next row (dec): K2tog, k3, k2tog (5 sts).
Next row: Purl.
Next row (dec): K2tog, k1, k2tog (3 sts).
Next row: Purl.
Next row: Sl1, k2tog, psso.
Fasten off.

TUSKS (MAKE 2)
With 4mm needles and B DOUBLED, cast on 17[19] sts.
Row 1 (dec): K2tog, k to last 2 sts, k2tog (15[17] sts).
Row 2: Purl.
Row 3 (dec): K2tog, k to last 2 sts, k2tog (13[15] sts).
Row 4: Purl.
Row 5 (dec): K5[6], sl1, k2tog, psso, k5[6] (11[13] sts).
Row 6: Purl.
Row 7: Kfb, k3[4], sl1, k2tog, psso, k3[4], kfb.
Row 8: Purl.
Rep last 2 rows 2[3] times more.
Next row (dec): K4[5], sl1, k2tog, psso, k4[5] (9[11] sts).
Next row: Purl.
Next row (dec): K2tog, k1[2], sl 1, k2tog, psso, k1[2], k2tog (5[7] sts).
Break yarn and thread through remaining sts. Fasten off.

MAKING UP
Using matching yarn, join the back seam.

With right sides together, sew the earflap facings to the earflaps, starting and finishing at the edge of the main section, leaving the overlapping cast-on edge open. Turn right side out and slipstitch the open edges to the inside of the main section.

With right sides together join the two ear pieces, leaving an opening. Turn the work right side out and stuff lightly, keeping the flattened shape, before closing. Attach the cast-on edges to each side of the hat with the pointed end of the ear facing down.

With right sides together, fold the trunk matching the seams. Stitch from the pointed V-shaped tip down the length of the seam, leaving the cast-on edge open. Stuff the trunk firmly, using a knitting needle to push the stuffing right into the ends. Attach the trunk to the hat, stitching all around the cast-on edge and work a few stitches near the end of the trunk to keep it in place at the top of the hat. Join the curved seam of the tusks. Stuff firmly and attach to either side of the trunk.

Make two twisted cords using A (see page 118), each measuring 8[12]in (20[30]cm) long, using 6[8] strands of yarn. Make two tassels (see page 119) measuring 4[5⅛]in (10[13]cm) long in A, and attach each to one end of the twisted cord, then stitch the other end of the cord to the tip of the earflap.

Using sewing thread, place the small black buttons over the larger white buttons and sew in place for the eyes.

LINING THE HAT
See pages 104–109 for how to make and attach a cosy fleece or knitted lining for your hat.

monkey

This cheeky chap is knitted in subtle shades of brown and grey bouclé yarn, which can easily be replaced by strong, contrasting colours and other textures to create an altogether different character.

MATERIALS
Any bouclé or textured chunky yarn
3[3] x 50g balls in brown (A)
1[1] x 50g balls in grey (B)
1 pair of 6mm (UK4:US10) needles
2 x brown ¾[⅞]in (2[2.25]cm) diameter buttons
2 x black ½[⅝]in (1.25[1.5]cm) diameter buttons
Stitch holder
Darning needle
Sewing needle
Black sewing thread
Small amount of toy stuffing
Thin card to make tassels

SIZES
To fit: child up to 8 years [adult]

TENSION
13 sts and 18 rows to 4in (10cm) over stocking
stitch using 6mm needles. Use larger or smaller
needles if necessary to obtain correct tension.

METHOD

The monkey's ears and face are knitted separately and attached to the finished main section. The lower part of the face is stuffed lightly to give shape. Nostrils are embroidered and the hat is finished with twisted cords and big tassels.

MAIN PIECE

First earflap

Both sizes

*Using 6mm needles and A, cast on 3 sts.
Row 1 (inc) (RS): Kfb, k1, kfb (5 sts).
Row 2: K2, p1, k2.
Row 3 (inc): Kfb, k3, kfb (7 sts).
Row 4: K2, p3, k2.
Row 5 (inc): Kfb, k5, kfb (9 sts).
Row 6: K2, p5, k2.
Row 7 (inc): Kfb, k7, kfb (11 sts).
Row 8: K2, p7, k2.
Row 9 (inc): Kfb, k9, kfb (13 sts).
Row 10: K2, p9, k2.
Row 11 (inc): Kfb, k11, kfb (15 sts).
Row 12: K2, p11, k2.

Adult size only

Row 13 (inc): Kfb, k13, kfb (17 sts).
Row 14: K2, p13, k2.

Both sizes

Row 15: Knit.
Row 16: As row 12[14].*
Break yarn and leave these sts on a holder.

Second earflap

Work as given for first earflap from * to *.

Next row: Cast on and k5 sts, knit across 15[17] sts of second earflap, turn, cast on 21 sts, turn, knit across 15[17] sts of first earflap, turn, cast on 5 sts (61[65] sts).
Next row (WS): K7, p11[13], k25, p11[13], k7.
Next row: Knit.
Rep last 2 rows once more and then starting with a purl row, work 19[21] rows in st st, ending with a WS row.

Shape crown

Row 1 (RS) (dec): K2tog, (k12[13], sl1, k2tog, psso) 3 times, k12[13], k2tog (53[57] sts).
Row 2: Purl.
Row 3 (dec): K2tog, (k10[11], sl1, k2tog, psso) 3 times, k10[11], k2tog (45[49] sts).
Row 4: Purl.
Row 5 (dec): K2tog, (k8[9], sl1, k2tog, psso) 3 times, k8[9], k2tog (37[41] sts).
Row 6: Purl.
Row 7 (dec): K2tog, (k6[7], sl1, k2tog, psso) 3 times, k6[7], k2tog (29[33] sts).
Row 8: Purl.
Row 9 (dec): K2tog, (k4[5], sl1, k2tog, psso) 3 times, k4[5], k2tog (21[25] sts).
Row 10: Purl.
Row 11 (dec): K2tog, (k2[3], sl1, k2tog, psso) 3 times, k2[3], k2tog (13[17] sts).

Adult size only

Row 12: Purl.
Row 13 (dec): K2tog, (k1, sl1, k2tog, psso) 3 times, k1, k2tog (9 sts).

Both sizes

Break yarn and thread through rem sts, draw up tight and fasten off.

EARFLAP FACING (MAKE 2)

Omit if you plan to add knitted lining
Using 6mm needles and A, cast on 3 sts and work as for earflaps.
Next: Rep rows 15 and 16 three more times.
Cast off loosely.

FACE

Starting at the chin, with 6mm needles and B, cast on 11[13] sts.
Row 1 (RS): Knit.
Row 2 (inc): Kfb, k9[11], kfb (13[15] sts).
Row 3: Knit.
Row 4 (inc): Kfb, k11[13], kfb (15[17] sts).

Mouth

Row 5: K2B, join in A and k11[13]A, k2B.
Row 6: K2B, k11[13]A, k2B.
Continue in B.
Rows 7–8: Knit.
Row 9 (dec): K2tog, k11[13], k2tog (13[15] sts).
Row 10: Knit.
Row 11 (dec): K2tog, k9[11] k2tog (11[13] sts).
Row 12: Knit.
Row 13 (inc): Kfb, k9[11], kfb (13[15] sts).
Row 14: Purl.
Row 15 (inc): Kfb, k5[6], kfb, k5[6], kfb (16[18] sts).
Row 16: Purl.

Adult size only

Row 17 (inc): Kfb, k16, kfb (20 sts).
Row 18: Purl.

Shape top of face
Both sizes
Each side is worked separately.
Row 19 (dec): K2tog, k4[6], k2tog, turn (6[8] sts).
Row 20: P6[8].
Row 21 (dec): K2tog, k2[4], k2tog, turn (4[6] sts).
Row 22: P4[6].
Cast off 4[6] sts. With RS facing rejoin yarn to remaining sts and work rows 19–22 to match first side.
Cast off.

OUTER EAR (MAKE 2)
Using 6mm needles and A, cast on 5[7] sts.
Row 1 (inc) (WS): Kfb, k3[5], kfb (7[9] sts).
Row 2 (RS): Knit.
Row 3 (inc): Kfb, k5[7], kfb (9[11] sts).
Both sizes
Work 10[12] rows in garter st.
Cast off.

INNER EAR (MAKE 2)
Work as for outer ear using yarn B.

MAKING UP
Using matching yarn, join the back seam.

With right sides together, sew the earflap facings to the earflaps, starting and finishing at the edge of the main section, leaving the overlapping cast-on edge open. Then, turn right side out and slipstitch the open edges to the inside of the main section.

Pin the face in position to the front of the hat with the cast-on stitches sitting just above the garter-stitch edge. Slipstitch around the shaped top and then work a row of backstitch across the middle at the narrowest part. Slipstitch the remaining half of the face to the main part leaving an opening. Stuff the lower half lightly to give the mouth and chin some shape. Close the opening and fasten off neatly.

With right sides together, sew the inner to the outer ear, leaving lower edge open. Turn right side out and lightly stuff, keeping the flattened shape. Join the cast-off edges. Attach the ears to the main section of the hat so they are in line with the top shaping of the face. Stitch all around the lower edges to help prevent them flopping over.

Make two twisted cords using A (see page 118), each measuring 8[12]in (20[30]cm) long, using 6[8] strands of yarn. Make two tassels (see page 119) measuring 4[5⅛]in (10[13]cm) long in B, and attach each to one end of the twisted cord, then stitch the other end of the cord to the tip of the earflap.

Embroider a couple of French knots (see page 119) for nostrils using yarn A. Using sewing thread, place the small black buttons over the larger brown buttons and sew in place for eyes.

LINING THE HAT
See pages 104–109 for how to make and attach a cosy fleece or knitted lining for your hat.

pig

Pretty in pink, this little piggy is knitted in soft, chunky
wool with a deep, turned-up rib to keep you extra cosy.
It is sure to chase away the winter blues.

MATERIALS

Debbie Bliss Rialto Chunky, 100% extra fine
    merino wool (65yds/60m per 50g ball)
3[3] x 50g balls in 016 Brighton Rock (A)
1 pair each of 6.5mm (UK3:US10.5) and 7mm
    (UK2:US10.5/11) needles
2 x white ¾[⅞]in (2[2.25]cm) diameter buttons
2 x black ½[⅝]in (1.25[1.5]cm) diameter buttons
2 small black buttons for nostrils measuring around
    ½in (1.25cm) across
Small amount of toy stuffing
Darning needle
Sewing needle
Black sewing thread

SIZES

To fit: child up to 8 years [adult]

TENSION

13 sts and 18 rows to 4in (10cm) over stocking
stitch using 7mm needles. Use larger or smaller
needles if necessary to obtain correct tension.

METHOD

The main part of the hat pattern is worked in the same format as the other projects, with a 2 x 2 rib replacing the earflaps. The ears, snout and tail are knitted separately and attached at the end.

MAIN PIECE

With 6.5mm needles and A, cast on 60[64] sts.
Work 4½[5]in (11.5[12.75]cm) in k2, p2 rib.
Change to 7mm needles.
Next row (inc) (RS): Kfb, k to end (61[65] sts).
Starting with a purl row, work in st st for 15[17] rows, ending with a WS row.
Shape crown
Row 1 (RS) (dec): K2tog, (k12[13], sl1, k2tog, psso) 3 times, k12[13], k2tog (53[57] sts).
Row 2: Purl.
Row 3 (dec): K2tog, (k10[11], sl1, k2tog, psso) 3 times, k10[11], k2tog (45[49] sts).
Row 4: Purl.
Row 5 (dec): K2tog, (k8[9], sl1, k2tog, psso) 3 times, k8[9], k2tog (37[41] sts).
Row 6: Purl.
Row 7 (dec): K2tog, (k6[7], sl1, k2tog, psso) 3 times, k6[7], k2tog (29[33] sts).
Row 8: Purl.
Row 9 (dec): K2tog, (k4[5], sl1, k2tog, psso) 3 times, k4[5], k2tog (21[25] sts).
Row 10: Purl.
Row 11 (dec): K2tog, (k2[3], sl1, k2tog, psso) 3 times, k2[3], k2tog (13[17] sts).

Adult size only
Row 12: Purl.
Row 13 (dec): K2tog, (k1, sl1, k2tog, psso) 3 times, k1, k2tog (9 sts).
Both sizes
Break yarn and thread through rem sts, draw up tight and fasten off.

EARS (MAKE 2)

With 7mm needles and A, cast on 6 sts.
Row 1 (inc): Kfb, k1, (kfb) twice, k1, kfb (10 sts).
Row 2 (inc): Kfb, k3, (kfb) twice, k3, kfb (14 sts).
Row 3 (inc): Kfb, k5, (kfb) twice, k5, kfb (18 sts).

Row 4 (inc): Kfb, k7, (kfb) twice, k7 kfb (22 sts).
Row 5 (inc): Kfb, k9, (kfb) twice, k9, kfb (26 sts).
Row 6 (inc): Kfb, k11, (kfb) twice, k11, kfb (30 sts).
Adult size only
Row 7 (inc): Kfb, k13, (kfb) twice, k13, kfb (34 sts).
Both sizes
Work 11[15] rows in garter st. Cast off.

SNOUT

Starting at back, with 7mm needles and A, cast on 5[7] sts.
Row 1 (inc): (K1, kfb) 2[3] times, k1 (7[10] sts).
Row 2: Purl.
Row 3 (inc): (K1, kfb[(kfb) twice]) 3 times, k1 (10[16] sts).
Adult size only
Row 4: Purl.
Row 5 (inc): K1, ((kfb) twice, k2) 3 times, (kfb) twice, k1 (24 sts).
Both sizes
Work 3[5] rows in st st.
Adult size only
Row 11 (dec): K1, ((k2tog) twice, k2) 3 times, (k2tog) twice, k1 (16 sts).
Row 12: Purl.
Both sizes
Row 13 (dec): (K1, k2tog[(k2tog) twice]) 3 times, k1 (7[10] sts).
Row 14: Purl.
Row 15 (dec): (K1, k2tog) 2[3] times, k1 (5[7] sts). Break yarn and thread through rem sts, draw up tight and fasten off.

CURLY TAIL
Both sizes
With 7mm needles and A, cast on 18[22] sts loosely by inserting the needle through the last stitch made, instead of in between the last 2 sts. Change to a 6.5mm needle and cast off tightly.

MAKING UP
With right sides together and using matching yarn, join the back seam from the top of the crown to halfway down the rib, then reversing the seam with wrong sides together for the turnback.

Join seam of the snout leaving an opening and stuff the piece lightly. Close the opening. Sew the small buttons to the snout, stitching right through to the back of the work, pulling tight on the thread to draw the nostrils in. Attach snout to the main part of the hat at the centre front, just above the garter-stitch border.

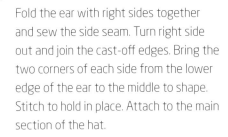

Fold the ear with right sides together and sew the side seam. Turn right side out and join the cast-off edges. Bring the two corners of each side from the lower edge of the ear to the middle to shape. Stitch to hold in place. Attach to the main section of the hat.

Using sewing thread, place the small black buttons over the larger white buttons and sew in place for the eyes.

Stitch tail to centre back of hat above the rib.

LINING THE HAT
See pages 104–109 for how to make and attach a cosy fleece or knitted lining for your hat.

fox

This foxy fellow, in his rusty-red coat, looks dashing with
his creamy features worked in intarsia. A shiny lurex
nose and soft mohair ears, along with fox-tail
pompom-tipped cords, all add to his character.

MATERIALS

Debbie Bliss Rialto Chunky, 100% merino wool
   (65yds/60m per 50g ball)
3[3] x 50g balls in 005 Burnt Umber (A)
1[2] x 50g balls in 003 Ecru (B)
*Debbie Bliss Angel, 76% superkid mohair, 24% silk
   (218yds/200m per 25g ball)
1[1] x 25g ball in 02 Black (C)
*Rowan Shimmer, 60% cupro, 40% polyester
   (191yds/175m per 25g ball)
1[1] x 25g ball in 095 Jet (D)
1 pair each of 7mm (UK2:US10.5/11) and 4mm
   (UK8:US6) needles
2 x brown ¾[⅞]in (2[2.25]cm) diameter buttons
2 x black ½[⅝]in (1.25[1.5]cm) diameter buttons
Small amount of toy stuffing
Stitch holder
Darning needle
Sewing needle
Black sewing thread
Thin card to make pompoms
*Use yarn DOUBLED

SIZES

To fit: child up to 8 years [adult]

TENSION

13 sts and 18 rows to 4in (10cm) over stocking
stitch using 7mm needles. Use larger or smaller
needles if necessary to obtain correct tension.

FOX CHART (8 rows x 61[65] sts)

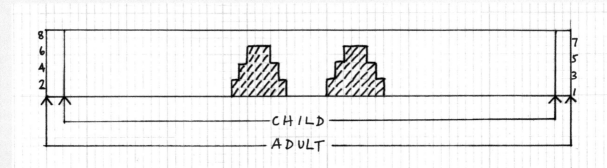

8
6
4
2

7
5
3
1

CHILD

ADULT

KEY

☐ YARN A
☒ YARN B

METHOD

The fox features are knitted in a simple intarsia pattern, giving a three-dimensional effect, with the little black nose and the ears worked separately.

MAIN PIECE

First earflap

Both sizes

*Using 7mm needles and A, cast on 3 sts.

Row 1 (inc) (RS): Kfb, k1, kfb (5 sts).
Row 2: K2, p1, k2.
Row 3 (inc): Kfb, k3, kfb (7 sts).
Row 4: K2, p3, k2.
Row 5 (inc): Kfb, k5, kfb (9 sts).
Row 6: K2, p5, k2.
Row 7 (inc): Kfb, k7, kfb (11 sts).
Row 8: K2, p7, k2.
Row 9 (inc): Kfb, k9, kfb (13 sts).
Row 10: K2, p9, k2.
Row 11 (inc): Kfb, k11, kfb (15 sts).
Row 12: K2, p11, k2.

Adult size only

Row 13 (inc): Kfb, k13, kfb (17 sts).
Row 14: K2, p13, k2.

Both sizes

Row 15: Knit.
Row 16: As row 12[14].*
Break yarn and leave these sts on a holder.

Second earflap

Work as given for first earflap from * to *.
The following is worked in intarsia:

Next row: Cast on and k 5 sts, knit across 15[17] sts of second earflap, turn. Join in B and cast on 21 sts, turn, knit across 15[17] sts of first earflap in A, turn, cast

on 5 sts in A (61[65] sts).
Next row (WS): K7A, p11[13]A, k2A, k21B, k2A, p11[13]A, k7A.
Next row: K20[22]A, k21B, k20[22]A.
Rep last 2 rows once more.
Next row (WS): P20[22]A, p21B, p20[22]A.
Next row: K20[22]A, k21B, k20[22]A.

Adult size only

Rep last 2 rows once more.

Both sizes

Rep the first of the previous 2 rows once again to end with a WS row.
Work following 8 rows from chart or as given below:

Row 1: K21[23]A, k7B, k5A, k7B, k21[23]A.
Row 2: P21[23]A, p7B, p5A, p7B, p21[23]A.
Row 3: K22[24]A, k5B, k7A, k5B, k22[24]A.
Row 4: P22[24]A, p5B, p7A, p5B, p22[24]A.
Row 5: K23[25]A, k3B, k9A, k3B, k23[25]A.
Row 6: P23[25]A, p3B, p9A, p3B, p23[25]A.
Row 7: K to end in A.
Row 8: P to end in A.
Rep last 2 rows 4 times more.

Shape crown

Row 1 (RS) (dec): K2tog, (k12[13], sl1, k2tog, psso) 3 times, k12[13], k2tog (53[57] sts).
Row 2: Purl.
Row 3 (dec): K2tog, (k10[11], sl1, k2tog, psso) 3 times, k10[11], k2tog (45[49] sts).
Row 4: Purl.
Row 5 (dec): K2tog, (k8[9], sl1, k2tog, psso) 3 times, k8[9], k2tog (37[41] sts).
Row 6: Purl.
Row 7 (dec): K2tog, (k6[7], sl1, k2tog, psso) 3 times, k6[7], k2tog (29[33] sts).
Row 8: Purl.
Row 9 (dec): K2tog, (k4[5], sl1, k2tog, psso) 3 times, k4[5], k2tog (21[25] sts).
Row 10: Purl.
Row 11 (dec): K2tog, (k2[3], sl1, k2tog, psso) 3 times, k2[3], k2tog (13[17] sts).

Adult size only

Row 12: Purl.
Row 13 (dec): K2tog, (k1, sl1, k2tog, psso) 3 times, k1, k2tog (9 sts).

Both sizes

Break yarn and thread through rem sts, draw up tight and fasten off.

EARFLAP FACING (MAKE 2)
Omit if you plan to add knitted lining
Using 7mm needles and A, cast on 3 sts
and work as for earflaps.
Next: Rep rows 15 and 16 three
more times.
Cast off loosely.

OUTER EAR (MAKE 2)
Both sizes
With 7mm needles and C DOUBLED, cast
on 3 sts.
Row 1 (inc): Kfb, k1, kfb (5 sts).
Row 2: Purl.
Row 3 (inc): Kfb, k3, kfb (7 sts).
Row 4: Purl.
Row 5 (inc): Kfb, k5, kfb (9sts).
Row 6: Purl.
Row 7 (inc): Kfb, k7, kfb (11 sts).
Row 8: Purl.
Row 9 (inc): Kfb, k9, kfb (13 sts).
Adult size only
Row 10: Purl.
Row 11 (inc): Kfb, k11, kfb (15 sts).
Row 12: Purl.
Row 13 (inc): Kfb, k13, kfb (17 sts).
Both sizes
Work 5 rows in st st.
Cast off.

INNER EAR (MAKE 2)
Both sizes
With 7mm needles and A, cast on 3 sts.
Row 1 (inc): Kfb, k1, kfb (5 sts).
Starting with p row, work 3 rows in st st.
Row 5 (inc): Kfb, k3, kfb (7 sts).
Work 3 rows in st st.

Row 9 (inc): Kfb, k5, kfb (9sts).
Work 5[3] rows st st.
Adult size only
Row 13 (inc): Kfb, k7, kfb (11 sts).
Work 5 rows in st st.
Both sizes
Cast off leaving a long length of yarn.

NOSE
Both sizes
Starting at the narrow base of the nose,
with 4mm needles and yarn D DOUBLED,
cast on 5 sts.
Row 1 (inc): (K1, kfb) twice, k1 (7 sts).
Row 2: Purl.
Row 3 (inc): K1, (kfb) twice, k1, (kfb)
twice, k1 (11 sts).
Adult size only
Row 4: Purl.
Row 5 (inc): K2, (kfb) twice, k3, (kfb)
twice, k2 (15 sts).
Both sizes
Cast off knitwise.

MAKING UP
Using matching yarn, join the back seam.

With right sides together, sew the
earflap facings to the earflaps, starting
and finishing at the edge of the main
section, leaving the overlapping cast-
on edge open. Turn right side out and
slipstitch the open edges to the inside
of the main section.

With right sides together sew the inner
to the outer ear, leaving lower edge open.
Turn right side out, positioning the inner
ear so it sits centrally with a slight overlap
each side of the larger outer piece. Lightly
stuff, keeping a flattened shape, and join
the cast-off edges. Bring the two corners
of each side from the lower edge of the
ear to the middle to form a bowl shape.
Stitch to hold in place. Attach to the main
section of the hat stitching all around the
lower shaped ear, which will help prevent
it flopping over.

Stitch side edges of the nose together
and, folding the piece with the seam at
centre back, join the lower narrow cast-
on edge, then the wider cast-off edge.
Attach the nose to the centre front of
the hat, just below the point where yarn
B meets yarn A at the centre front.

Make two twisted cords using A (see page
118), each measuring 8[12]in (20[30]
cm) long, using 6[8] strands of yarn. Make
two 2[2⅜]in (5[6]cm) pompoms in B (see
page 118) and attach each to one end
of the twisted cord, then stitch the other
end of the cord to the tip of the earflap.
Using sewing thread, place the small black
buttons over the larger brown buttons
and sew in place for the eyes.

LINING THE HAT
See pages 104–109 for how to make
and attach a cosy fleece or knitted lining
for your hat.

lion

The lion's splendid mane is made by working a fur-like looped stitch into the pattern of the main section of the hat. It creates an open weave, yet still gives plenty of warmth to the wearer.

MATERIALS

Erika Knight Fat Maxi Wool, 100% pure British wool
(87yds/80m per 100g ball)
3[3] x 100g balls in 20 Artisan (A)
Oddment of chunky yarn in black (B)
1 pair each of 12mm (UK-:US17) and 7mm
(UK2:US10.5) needles
2 x brown ¾[⅞]in (2[2.25]cm) diameter buttons
2 x black ½[⅝]in (1.25[1.5]cm) diameter buttons
Stitch holder
Darning needle
Sewing needle
Black sewing thread
Thin card to make pompoms

SIZES

To fit: child up to 8 years [adult]

TENSION

8 sts and 12 rows to 4in (10cm) over stocking
stitch using 12mm needles. Use larger or smaller
needles if necessary to obtain correct tension.

SPECIAL ABBREVIATIONS

ML: Make loop by winding the yarn around both the
right-hand needle and left forefinger clockwise and
then the right-hand needle alone anticlockwise, as
normal, to work the stitch. The loop is secured by
knitting the two loops formed together. See page
116 for full instructions and illustrations.

METHOD

The lion's mane is knitted into the main section of the hat, starting with the earflaps. The looped stitches change the tension of the work but add to the fullness of the mane. The ears and nose are worked separately and attached to the hat, with button eyes and pompom-tipped cords.

MAIN PIECE

First earflap
Both sizes
*With 12mm needles and A, cast on 3 sts.
Row 1 (inc) (RS): Kfb, k1, kfb (5 sts).
Row 2: K2, p1, k2.
Row 3 (inc): Kfb, (ML) 3 times, kfb (7 sts).
Row 4: K2, p3, k2.
Row 5 (inc): Kfb, (ML) 5 times, kfb (9 sts).
Row 6: K2, p5, k2.
Adult size only
Row 7 (inc): Kfb, (ML) 7 times, kfb (11 sts).
Row 8: K2, p7, k2.
Both sizes
Row 9: K2, (ML) 5[7] times, k2.
Row 10: As row 6[8].*
Break yarn and leave these sts on a holder.

Second earflap
Work as given for first earflap from * to *.
Next row: Cast on and k 4 sts, (K2, (ML) 5[7] times, k2) of second earflap, turn, cast on 15 sts, turn, (K2, (ML) 5[7] times, k2) of first earflap, turn, cast on 4 sts (41[45] sts).
Next row (WS): K6, p5[7], k19, p5[7], k6.
Next row: K6, (ML) 5[7] times, k19, (ML)

5[7] times, k6.
Rep first of last 2 rows once more.
Next row: K1, (ML) 12[14] times, k15, (ML) 12[14] times, k1.
Next row: P to end.
Rep last 2 rows twice[three] times.
Shape face
Row 1: K1, (ML) 13[15] times, k13, (ML) 13[15] times, k1.
Row 2: P to end.
Row 3: K1, (ML) 14[16] times, k11, (ML) 14[16] times, k1.
Row 4: P to end.
Row 5: K1, (ML) 15[17] times, k9, (ML) 15[17] times, k1.
Row 6: P to end.
Row 7: K1, (ML) to last st, k1.
Shape crown
Row 1 (dec): P0[1], p2tog, (p1, p2tog) to end (27[30] sts).
Row 2: K1, (ML) to last st, k1.
Row 3 (dec): P1[0], (p2tog) to end (14[15] sts).
Break yarn and thread through rem sts, draw up tight and fasten off.

EARFLAP FACINGS (MAKE 2)

Omit if you plan to add knitted lining
Both sizes
With 12mm needles and A, cast on 3 sts.
Row 1 (inc) (RS): Kfb, k1, kfb (5 sts).
Row 2: K2, p1, k2.
Row 3 (inc): Kfb, k3, kfb (7 sts).
Row 4: K2, p3, k2.
Row 5 (inc): Kfb, k5, kfb (9 sts).
Row 6: K2, p5, k2.
Adult size only
Row 7 (inc): Kfb, k7, kfb (11 sts).

Row 8: K2, p7, k2.
Both sizes
Row 9: Knit.
Row 10: As row 6[8].
Next: Rep rows 9 and 10 three more times.
Cast off loosely.

EARS (MAKE 2)

Using 12mm needles and A, cast on 6[7] sts.
Row 1: Knit.
*Row 2 (inc): Kfb, k4[5], kfb (8[9] sts).
Adult size only
Row 3: Knit.
Row 4 (inc): Kfb, k7, kfb (11 sts).
Both sizes
Knit 5 rows.
Adult size only
Next row: Knit.
Next row (dec): K2tog, k7, k2tog (9 sts).
Next row: Knit.
Both sizes
Next row (dec): K2tog, k4[5], k2tog (6[7] sts).
Next row: Knit.*
Rep from * to *.
Cast off.

NOSE

Both sizes
Starting at the narrow base of the nose, with 7mm needles and yarn B, cast on 3 sts.
Row 1 (WS): Purl.
Row 2 (inc): Kfb, k1, kfb (5 sts).
Row 3: Purl
Row 4 (inc): Kfb, (k1, kfb) twice (8 sts).
Row 5: Purl.

Adult size only
Row 6: Kfb, k6, kfb (10 sts).
Row 7: Purl.
Row 8 (dec): K2tog, k6, k2tog (8 sts).
Row 9: Purl.
Both sizes
Row 10 (dec): K2tog (k1, k2tog) twice (5 sts).
Row 11: Purl.
Row 12 (dec): K2tog, k1, k2tog (3 sts).
Cast off.

MAKING UP

Make sure the loops don't get caught up in the stitches when making up the hat. Using matching yarn, join the back seam.

With right sides together, sew the earflap facings to the earflaps, starting and finishing at the edge of the main section, leaving the overlapping cast-on edge open. Turn right side out and pin in place, easing in the fullness of the looped

earflap edges to match the facings. Slipstitch the open edges to the inside of the main section.

Fold ear piece with right sides together and join the shaped side seams, leaving the cast-on and cast-off edges open. Turn right sides out, stuff lightly then close the seam. Fold the lower edge, bringing each corner to the centre to shape the ear and stitch in place. Attach the finished ears to the hat.

Fold nose with wrong sides together, matching the narrow cast-on and cast-off edges. Join the seams neatly. Attach the nose to the centre front of the hat, with the narrow end sitting just above the garter-stitch edge.

Make two twisted cords using A (see page 118), each measuring 8[12]in (20[30]cm) long, using 4[6] strands of

yarn. Make two 2[2³⁄₈]in (5[6]cm) pompoms in A (see page 118) and attach each to one end of the twisted cord, then stitch the other end of the cord to the earflap tip.

Using sewing thread, place the small black buttons over the larger brown buttons and sew onto the lion's face for the eyes.

LINING THE HAT
See pages 104–109 for how to make and attach a cosy fleece or knitted lining for your hat.

mouse

By putting together yarns of varied textures, the mouse
is given a tactile quality and interesting finish. Be sure
to stitch the large ears all around the lower edge
when attaching to the hat, so they don't flop.

MATERIALS

Wendy Merino Chunky, 100% merino wool
    (71yds/65m per 50g ball)
3[3] x 50g balls in 2477 Soot (A)
Wendy Sorrento DK, 45% cotton, 55% acrylic
    (159yds/145m per 50g ball)
1[1] x 50g ball in 2405 Pale Pink (B)
Any textured or bouclé chunky yarn
1[1] x 50g ball in light grey (C)
Oddment of black DK yarn (D)
1 pair each of 7mm (UK2:US10.5/11) and
    4mm (UK8:US6) needles
2 x white ¾[⅞]in (2[2.25]cm) diameter buttons
2 x black ½[⅝]in (1.25[1.5]cm) diameter buttons
Stitch holder
Darning needle
Sewing needle
Black sewing thread
Thin card to make pompoms
Small amount of toy stuffing

SIZES

To fit: child up to 8 years [adult]

TENSION

13 sts and 18 rows to 4in (10cm) over stocking
stitch using 7mm needles. Use larger or smaller
needles if necessary to obtain correct tension.

METHOD

The main part of the hat is knitted first, beginning with the earflaps. Ears, cheeks and the bobble nose are worked separately and stitched to the hat after the back seam is joined and the ear facings attached. Whiskers are embroidered across the cheeks.

MAIN PIECE

First earflap

Both sizes

*Using 7mm needles and A, cast on 3 sts.

Row 1 (inc) (RS): Kfb, k1, kfb (5 sts).

Row 2: K2, p1, k2.

Row 3 (inc): Kfb, k3, kfb (7 sts).

Row 4: K2, p3, k2.

Row 5 (inc): Kfb, k5, kfb (9 sts).

Row 6: K2, p5, k2.

Row 7 (inc): Kfb, k7, kfb (11 sts).

Row 8: K2, p7, k2.

Row 9 (inc): Kfb, k9, kfb (13 sts).

Row 10: K2, p9, k2.

Row 11 (inc): Kfb, k11, kfb (15 sts).

Row 12: K2, p11, k2.

Adult size only

Row 13 (inc): Kfb, k13, kfb (17 sts).

Row 14: K2, p13, k2.

Both sizes

Row 15: Knit.

Row 16: As row 12[14].*

Break yarn and leave these sts on a holder.

Second earflap

Work as given for first earflap from * to *.

Next row: Cast on and k 5 sts, knit across 15[17] sts of second earflap, turn, cast on 21 sts, turn, knit across 15[17] sts of first earflap, turn, cast on 5 sts (61[65] sts).

Next row (WS): K7, p11[13], k25, p11[13], k7.

Next row: Knit.

Rep last 2 rows once more and then starting with a purl row, work 19[21] rows in st st, ending with a WS row.

Shape crown

Row 1 (RS) (dec): K2tog, (k12[13], sl1, k2tog, psso) 3 times, k12[13], k2tog (53[57] sts).

Row 2: Purl.

Row 3 (dec): K2tog, (k10[11], sl1, k2tog, psso) 3 times, k10[11], k2tog (45[49] sts).

Row 4: Purl.

Row 5 (dec): K2tog, (k8[9], sl1, k2tog, psso) 3 times, k8[9], k2tog (37[41] sts).

Row 6: Purl.

Row 7 (dec): K2tog, (k6[7], sl1, k2tog, psso) 3 times, k6[7], k2tog (29[33] sts).

Row 8: Purl.

Row 9 (dec): K2tog, (k4[5], sl1, k2tog, psso) 3 times, k4[5], k2tog (21[25] sts).

Row 10: Purl.

Row 11 (dec): K2tog, (k2[3], sl1, k2tog, psso) 3 times, k2[3], k2tog (13[17] sts).

Adult size only

Row 12: Purl.

Row 13 (dec): K2tog, (k1, sl1, k2tog, psso) 3 times, k1, k2tog (9 sts).

Both sizes

Break yarn and thread through rem sts, draw up tight and fasten off.

EARFLAP FACING (MAKE 2)

Omit if you plan to add knitted lining

Using 7mm needles and A, cast on 3 sts and work rows 1 to 16 of pattern for earflaps.

Next: Rep rows 15 and 16 three more times.

Cast off loosely.

EARS (MAKE 4)

Using 7mm needles and A, cast on 7[9] sts.

Rows 1-2: Knit.

Row 3 (inc) (WS): Kfb, k5[7], kfb (9[11] sts).

Row 4 (RS): Knit.

Row 5 (inc): Kfb, k7[9], kfb (11[13] sts).

Row 6: Knit.

Row 7 (inc): Kfb, k9[11], kfb (13[15] sts).

Rows 8-16: Knit.

Adult size only

Rows 17-18: Knit.

Both sizes
Row 19 (dec): K2tog, k9[11], k2tog (11[13] sts).
Row 20: Knit.
Row 21 (dec): K2tog, k7[9], k2tog (9[11] sts).
Row 22: Knit.
Row 23 (dec): K2tog, k5[7], k2tog (7[9] sts).
Rows 24: Knit.
Row 25 (dec): K2tog, k3[5], k2tog (5[7] sts).
Cast off.

INNER EARS (MAKE 2)

With 4mm needles and B, cast on 7[9] sts and work rows 1 to 24 of ear pattern. Cast off leaving a long length of yarn.

CHEEKS (MAKE 2)

Both sizes
Using 7mm needles and C, cast on 7 sts.
Row 1 (inc): Kfb, k5, kfb (9 sts).
Row 2: Knit.
Row 3 (inc): Kfb, k7, kfb (11 sts).
Rows 4-5: Knit.
Adult size only
Rows 6-7: Knit.
Both sizes
Row 8 (dec): K2tog, k7, k2tog (9 sts).
Row 9: Knit.
Row 10 (dec): K2tog, k5, k2tog (7 sts).
Cast off.

NOSE

Both sizes
Starting at the narrow base of the nose, with 4mm needles and D, cast on 3 sts.
Row 1 (inc): Kfb, k1, kfb (5 sts).
Row 2 (inc): K1, (kfb) 3 times, k1 (8 sts).
Adult size only
Row 3 (inc): (K1, kfb) 4 times (12 sts).
Both sizes
Knit 7[9] rows.
Adult size only
Row 13 (dec): (K1, k2tog) 4 times (8 sts).
Both sizes
Next row (dec): K1, (k2tog) 3 times, k1 (5 sts).
Next row (dec): K2tog, k1, k2tog (3 sts).
Cast off leaving a long length of yarn. Run a gathering st around the edge and draw up to gather, stuffing the piece to make a ball shape before fastening off.

MAKING UP

Using matching yarn, join the back seam.

With right sides together, sew the earflap facings to the earflaps, starting and finishing at the edge of the main section, leaving the overlapping cast-on edge open. Turn right side out and slipstitch the open edges to the inside of the main section.

With right sides together join the two ear pieces, leaving lower, cast-on edge open. Turn right side out and stuff lightly before stitching together the cast-on edges. Sew the pink inner pieces to the middle of the ears. Attach the ears in place on the main section of the hat, stitching all around the lower edges to prevent them flopping over.

Sew cheeks to face, just above the garter-stitch edge, setting them close together.

Stitch the nose in between the top shaping of the cheeks and work long whiskery stitches in yarn D across each cheek.

Make two twisted cords in A (see page 118) measuring 8[12]in (20[30]cm), using 6[8] strands of yarn. Make two 2[2⅜]in (5[6]cm) pompoms in C (see page 118) and attach each to one end of the twisted cord, then stitch the other end of the cord to the tip of the earflap.

Using sewing thread, place the small black buttons over the larger white buttons and sew in place for the eyes.

LINING THE HAT

See pages 104–109 for how to make and attach a cosy fleece or knitted lining for your hat.

rabbit

Spring is in the air and this floppy-eared bunny rabbit
will keep the breezes at bay. His fluffy cheeks,
pink nose and two bunny-tail pompoms
add to his cuddly charm.

MATERIALS

Rowan Felted Tweed Chunky, 50% merino wool,
    25% alpaca, 25% viscose (55yds/50m per
    50g ball)
4[4] x 50g balls in 280 Sand (A)
1[1] x 50g ball in 290 Candy (B)
Rowan Purelife British Sheep Breeds Boucle, 100%
    British wool (66yds/60m per 100g ball)
1[1] x 100g ball in 220 Blue Faced Leicester/ecru (C)
1 pair each of 6.5mm (UK3:US10.5) and
    8mm (UK0:US11) needles
2 x white ⅞in (2.25cm) diameter buttons
2 x black ⅝in (1.5cm) diameter buttons
Stitch holder
Darning needle
Sewing needle
Black sewing thread
Thin card to make pompoms

SIZES

To fit: child up to 8 years [adult]

TENSION

12½ sts and 17½ rows to 4in (10cm)
over stocking stitch using 6.5mm needles.
Use larger or smaller needles if necessary
to obtain correct tension.

METHOD
The long bunny ears, cheeks and nose are
knitted separately and stitched in place
to the finished hat. The main part begins
with the earflaps to warm the wearer's
own ears. The hat is finished with button
eyes and pompoms to decorate the ends
of the twisted cords.

MAIN PIECE
First earflap
Both sizes
*Using 6.5mm needles and A, cast on
3 sts.
Row 1 (inc) (RS): Kfb, k1, kfb (5 sts).
Row 2: K2, p1, k2.
Row 3 (inc): Kfb, k3, kfb (7 sts).
Row 4: K2, p3, k2.
Row 5 (inc): Kfb, k5, kfb (9 sts).
Row 6: K2, p5, k2.
Row 7 (inc): Kfb, k7, kfb (11 sts).
Row 8: K2, p7, k2.
Row 9 (inc): Kfb, k9, kfb (13 sts).
Row 10: K2, p9, k2.
Row 11 (inc): Kfb, k11, kfb (15 sts).
Row 12: K2, p11, k2.
Adult size only
Row 13 (inc): Kfb, k13, kfb (17 sts).
Row 14: K2, p13, k2.
Both sizes
Row 15: Knit.
Row 16: As row 12[14].*
Break yarn and leave these sts
on a holder.
Second earflap
Work as given for first earflap from * to *.
Next row: Cast on and knit 5 sts, knit
across 15[17] sts of second earflap, turn,

cast on 21 sts, turn, knit across 15[17]
sts of first earflap, turn, cast on 5 sts
(61[65] sts).
Next row (WS): K7, p11[13], k25,
p11[13], k7.
Next row: Knit.
Rep last 2 rows once more and then
starting with a purl row, work 19[21]
rows in st st, ending with a WS row.
Shape crown
Row 1 (RS) (dec): K2tog, (k12[13], sl1,
k2tog, psso) 3 times, k12[13], k2tog
(53[57] sts).
Row 2: Purl.
Row 3 (dec): K2tog, (k10[11], sl1, k2tog,

psso) 3 times, k10[11], k2tog (45[49] sts).
Row 4: Purl.
Row 5 (dec): K2tog, (k8[9], sl1, k2tog,
psso) 3 times, k8[9], k2tog (37[41] sts).
Row 6: Purl.
Row 7 (dec): K2tog, (k6[7], sl1, k2tog,
psso) 3 times, k6[7], k2tog (29[33] sts).
Row 8: Purl.
Row 9 (dec): K2tog, (k4[5], sl1, k2tog,
psso) 3 times, k4[5], k2tog (21[25] sts).
Row 10: Purl.
Row 11 (dec): K2tog, (k2[3], sl1, k2tog,
psso) 3 times, k2[3], k2tog (13[17] sts).
Adult size only
Row 12: Purl.
Row 13 (dec): K2tog, (k1, sl1, k2tog,
psso) 3 times, k1, k2tog (9 sts).
Both sizes
Break yarn and thread through rem sts,
draw up tight and fasten off.

EARFLAP FACING (MAKE 2)
Omit if you plan to add knitted lining
Using 6.5mm needles and A, cast on
3 sts and work rows 1 to 16 of pattern
for earflaps.
Next: Rep rows 15 and 16 three
more times. Cast off loosely.

OUTER EAR (MAKE 2)
Both sizes
With 6.5mm needles and A, cast on 3 sts.
Row 1 (inc): Kfb, k1, kfb (5 sts).
Row 2: Purl.
Row 3 (inc): Kfb, k3, kfb (7 sts).
Row 4: Purl.
Row 5 (inc): Kfb, k5, kfb (9 sts).
Row 6: Purl.

Row 7 (inc): Kfb, k7, kfb (11 sts).
Row 8: Purl.
Row 9 (inc): Kfb, k9, kfb (13 sts).
Adult size only
Row 10: Purl.
Row 11 (inc): Kfb, k11, kfb (15 sts).
Row 12: Purl.
Row 13 (inc): Kfb, k13, kfb (17 sts).
Both sizes
Work 17 rows in st st.
Cast off.

INNER EAR (MAKE 2)
Both sizes
With 6.5mm needles and B, cast on 3 sts.
Row 1 (inc): Kfb, k1, kfb (5 sts).
Starting with p row, work 3 rows in st st.
Row 5 (inc): Kfb, k3, kfb (7 sts).
Work 3 rows in st st.
Row 9 (inc): Kfb, k5, kfb (9 sts).
Adult size only
Work 3 rows st st.
Row 13 (inc): Kfb, k7, kfb (11 sts).
Both sizes
Work 17 rows in st st.
Cast off leaving a long length of yarn.

CHEEKS (MAKE 2)
Both sizes
Using 8mm needles and C, cast on 3 sts.
Row 1 (inc): Kfb, k1, kfb (5 sts).
Row 2: Knit.
Row 3 (inc): Kfb, k3, kfb (7 sts).
Rows 4–5: Knit.
Row 6 (dec): K2tog, k3, k2tog (5 sts).
Row 7: Knit.
Row 8 (dec): K2tog, k1, k2tog (3 sts).
Cast off.

NOSE
Both sizes
With 6.5mm needles and B, cast on 5 sts.
Work 5 rows in st st.
Cast off knitwise.

MAKING UP
Using matching yarn, join the back seam.

With right sides together, sew the earflap facings to the earflaps, starting and finishing at the edge of the main section, leaving the overlapping cast-on edge open. Turn right side out and slipstitch the open edges to the inside of the main section.

With right sides together sew the inner to the outer ear, leaving lower edge open. Turn right sides out, positioning the inner ear so it sits centrally with a slight overlap each side of the larger outer piece. Join the cast-off edges. Bring the two corners of each side from the lower edge of the ear to the middle to shape. Stitch to hold in place. Attach to the main section of the hat.

Sew cheeks to face, just above the garter-stitch edge, setting them close together.

Fold nose diagonally and join edges to form a triangular shape. With the folded edge at the top, attach nose to centre front of hat, in between the top shaping of the cheeks.

Make two twisted cords (see page 118) measuring 8[12]in (20[30]cm) long in A, using 6[8] strands of yarn. Make two 2[2⅜] in (5[6]cm) pompoms (see page 118) in C and attach each to one end of the twisted cord, then stitch the other end of the cord to the tip of the earflap.

Using sewing thread, place the small black buttons over the larger white buttons and sew in place for the eyes.

LINING THE HAT
See pages 104–109 for how to make and attach a cosy fleece or knitted lining for your hat.

cat

The soft, textured bouclé wool gives this cute kitty
an even cuddlier feel and using the super-chunky yarn
will also make the hat very quick to knit – purrr-fect!

MATERIALS

Rowan Purelife British Sheep Breeds Bouclé, 100%
    British wool (66yds/60m per 100g ball)
1[1] x 100g ball in 223 Dark Brown Masham (A)
1[1] x 100g ball in 220 Blue Faced Leicester/ecru (B)
Oddment of DK yarn in pink (C)
1 pair each of 7.5mm (UK1:US10.5), 8mm
    (UK0:US11) and 4mm (UK8:US6) needles
2 x dark brown ⅞in (2.25cm) diameter buttons
2 x black ⅝in (1.5cm) diameter buttons
Stitch holder
Darning needle
Sewing needle
Black sewing thread
Black embroidery thread
Small amount of toy stuffing

SIZES

To fit: child up to 8 years [adult]

TENSION

8½ sts and 13 rows to 4in (10cm) over stocking
stitch using 8mm needles. Use larger or smaller
needles if necessary to obtain correct tension.

METHOD

The cat hat is worked in intarsia pattern, with the cheeks knitted separately and stitched on to the face to give a little shape to the features. Whiskers are embroidered using long stitches.

MAIN PIECE

With 7.5mm needles and A, cast on 41[45] sts.

Work 3 rows in garter st. Change to 8mm needles.

The following is worked in intarsia:

Next row (RS): K13[15]A, k15B, k13[15]A.

Next row: P13[15]A, p15B, p13[15]A.

Rep last 2 rows 2[3] times.

Work following 8 rows from chart or as given below:

Row 1: K14[16]A, k13B, k14[16]A.
Row 2: P14[16]A, p13B, p14[16]A.
Row 3: K15[17]A, k11B, k15[17]A.
Row 4: P15[17]A, p11B, p15[17]A.
Row 5: K16[18]A, k9B, k16[18]A.
Row 6: P16[18]A, p9B, p16[18]A.
Row 7: K to end in A.
Row 8: P to end in A.

Shape crown

Row 1 (dec): K2tog, (k7[8], sl1, k2tog, psso) 3 times, k7[8], k2tog (33[37] sts).
Row 2: Purl.
Row 3 (dec): K2tog, (k5[6], sl1, k2tog, psso) 3 times, k5[6], k2tog (25[29] sts).
Row 4: Purl.
Row 5 (dec): K2tog, (k3[4], sl1, k2tog, psso) 3 times, k3[4], k2tog (17[21] sts).
Row 6: Purl.
Row 7 (dec): K2tog, (k1[2], sl1, k2tog, psso) 3 times, k1[2], k2tog (9[13] sts).
Break yarn and thread through rem sts, draw up tight and fasten off.

OUTER EAR (MAKE 2)
Both sizes

With 8mm needles and A, cast on 3 sts.
Row 1 (inc): Kfb, k1, kfb (5 sts).
Row 2: Purl.
Row 3 (inc): Kfb, k3, kfb (7 sts).
Row 4: Purl.
Row 5 (inc): Kfb, k5, kfb (9 sts).
Adult size only
Row 6: Purl.
Row 7 (inc): Kfb, k7, kfb (11 sts).
Both sizes
Work 3 rows in st st. Cast off.

INNER EAR (MAKE 2)
Both sizes

With 8mm needles and B, cast on 3 sts.
Row 1: Knit.
Row 2: Purl.
Row 3 (inc): Kfb, k1, kfb (5 sts).
Starting with p row, work 5[3] rows in st st.
Adult size only
Row 7 (inc): Kfb, k3, kfb (7 sts).
Work 3 rows in st st.
Both sizes
Cast off leaving a long length of yarn.

CHEEKS (MAKE 2)
Both sizes

Using 8mm needles and B, cast on 3 sts.
Row 1 (inc): Kfb, k1, kfb (5 sts).
Row 2: Knit.
Row 3 (inc): Kfb, k3, kfb (7 sts).
Row 4: Knit.
Adult size only
Row 5: Knit.
Both sizes
Row 6 (dec): K2tog, k3, k2tog (5 sts).
Row 7: Knit.
Row 8 (dec): K2tog, k1, k2tog (3 sts).
Cast off.

CAT CHART (8 rows x 41[45] sts)

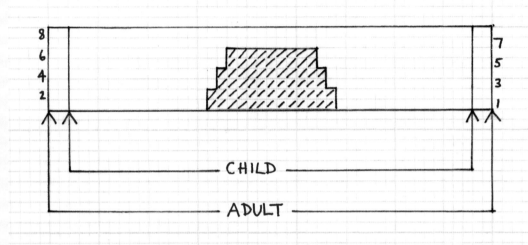

KEY

☐ YARN A
▨ YARN B

NOSE

Both sizes

Starting at the narrow base of the nose, with 4mm needles and yarn C, cast on 3 sts.

Row 1 (inc): Kfb, k1, kfb (5 sts).

Row 2: Purl

Row 3 (inc): (K1, kfb) twice, k1 (7 sts).

Row 4: Purl

Row 5 (inc): K1, (kfb) twice, k1, (kfb) twice, k1 (11 sts).

Adult size only

Row 6: Purl.

Row 7 (inc): K2, (kfb) twice, k3, (kfb) twice, k2 (15 sts).

Both sizes

Cast off knitwise.

MAKING UP

Using matching yarn, join the back seam.

With right sides together sew the inner to the outer ear, leaving lower edge open. Turn right side out, positioning the inner ear so it sits centrally with a slight overlap each side of the larger outer piece. Stuff lightly, keeping the shape flat and join the cast-off edges. Attach to the main section of the hat.

Sew cheeks to face, just over the garter-stitch edge, setting them close together. Stitch the side edges of the nose together and, folding the piece with the seam at centre back, join the cast-off edge. With the wide cast-off edge at the top, attach the nose to the face, in between the top shaping of the cheeks.

Embroider whiskers on the cheeks by working long stitches in black embroidery thread or yarn (see page 119). Using sewing thread, place the small black buttons over the larger brown buttons and sew in place for the eyes.

LINING THE HAT

See pages 104–109 for how to make and attach a cosy fleece or knitted lining for your hat.

dog

This loyal pooch with his playful puppy eye patch
and long ears lends purpose to the tracker-style hat,
which can be worn with button-up ears as an alerted
hound or ears down as the earnest investigator.

MATERIALS

Rowan Purelife British Sheep Breeds Chunky
    Undyed, 100% British wool (120yds/110m per
    100g ball)
1[1] x 100g ball in 950 Blue Faced Leicester (A)
1[1] x 100g ball in 952 Mid Brown Jacob (B)
*Rowan Shimmer, 60% cupro, 40% polyester
    (191yds/175m per 25g ball)
1[1] x 25g ball in 095 Jet (C)
1 pair each of 7mm (UK2:US10.5/11) and
    4mm (UK8:US6) needles
4 x cream or white ⅞in (2.25cm) diameter buttons
2 x black ⅝in (1.5cm) diameter buttons
Darning needle
Sewing needle
Cream or white thread
Black sewing thread
*Use Rowan Shimmer DOUBLED

SIZES

To fit: child up to 8 years [adult]

TENSION

13 sts and 18 rows to 4in (10cm) over stocking
stitch using 7mm needles. Use larger or smaller
needles if necessary to obtain correct tension.

METHOD

The main section starts with knitting the ear facings, then working them into the crown of the hat. The ears, eye patch and shiny, wet-look nose are knitted separately and stitched on. The long ears can be buttoned up and another set of buttons are attached for the eyes.

EAR FACINGS (MAKE 2)
Both sizes
Using 7mm needles and A, cast on 5 sts.
Row 1 (RS) (inc): Kfb, k3, kfb (7 sts).
Row 2 (inc): Kfb, k5, kfb (9 sts).
Row 3 (inc): Kfb, k7, kfb (11 sts).
Row 4 (inc): Kfb, k9, kfb (13 sts).
Adult size only
Row 5 (inc): Kfb, k11, kfb (15 sts).
Both sizes
Continue in garter st (k every row) until work measures 4¾[6]in (12[15]cm) from cast-on edge, ending with a WS row. Break yarn and leave sts on a holder.

MAIN PIECE
Using 7mm needles and A, cast on 8 sts, turn and k across 13[15] sts of one ear facing, turn and cast on 19 sts, turn and k across 13[15] sts of other ear facing, turn and cast on 8 sts (61[65] sts). Work 3 rows in garter st.
Beg with a k row, work in st st for 20[22] rows, ending with a WS row.
Shape crown
Row 1 (RS) (dec): K2tog, k11[12], sl1, k2tog, psso, (k13[14], sl1, k2tog, psso) twice, k11[12], k2tog (53[57] sts).
Row 2: Purl.
Row 3 (dec): K2tog, k9[10], sl1, k2tog, psso, (k11[12], sl1, k2tog, psso) twice, k9[10], k2tog (45[49] sts).
Row 4: Purl.
Row 5 (dec): K2tog, k7[8], sl1, k2tog, psso, (k9[10], sl1, k2tog, psso) twice, k7[8], k2tog (37[41] sts).
Row 6: Purl.
Row 7 (dec): K2tog, k5[6], sl1, k2tog, psso, (k7[8], sl1, k2tog, psso) twice, k5[6], k2tog (29[33] sts).
Row 8: Purl.
Row 9 (dec): K2tog, k3[4], sl1, k2tog, psso, (k5[6], sl1, k2tog, psso) twice, k3[4], k2tog (21[25] sts).
Row 10: Purl.
Row 11 (dec): K2tog, k1[2], sl1, k2tog, psso, (k3[4], sl1, k2tog, psso) twice, k1[2], k2tog (13[17] sts).
Adult size only
Row 12: Purl.
Row 13 (dec): K2tog, sl1, k2tog, psso, (k2, sl1, k2tog, psso) twice, k2tog (9 sts).

Both sizes
Break yarn and thread through rem sts, draw up tight and fasten off.

EARS (MAKE 2)
Both sizes
Using 7mm needles and B, cast on 3 sts, (pass previous st over st just made, slipping it off the needle, cast on 1) 3 times to make buttonhole.
Row 1 (WS): K1, turn, cast on 3 sts, turn, k1 (5 sts).
Row 2: (inc): Kfb, k3, kfb (7 sts).
Row 3 (inc): Kfb, k5, kfb (9 sts).
Row 4 (inc): Kfb, k7, kfb (11 sts).
Row 5 (inc): Kfb, k9, kfb (13 sts).
Adult size only
Row 6 (inc): Kfb, k11, kfb (15 sts).
Both sizes
Continue in garter st until work measures 7[8¼]in (18[21]cm) from cast-on edge of row 1, ending with a WS row.
Shape top
Next row (dec): K1, k2tog, k to last 3 sts, k2tog, k1.
Next row: Knit.
Rep last 2 rows until 9 sts rem, then rep the first of the last 2 rows twice more (5 sts).
Next row (dec): K1, sl1, k2tog, psso, k1 (3 sts).
Cast off 3 sts.

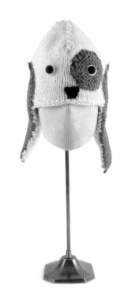

NOSE

Both sizes

Starting at the narrow base of the nose, with 4mm needles and yarn C DOUBLED, cast on 7 sts.

Row 1 (RS): Knit.

Row 2: Purl.

Row 3 (inc): K1, (kfb) twice, k1, (kfb) twice, k1 (11 sts).

Adult size only

Row 4: Purl.

Row 5 (inc): K2, (kfb) twice, k3, (kfb) twice, k2 (15 sts).

Both sizes

Cast off knitwise.

PATCH

Using 7mm needles and B, cast on 5[7] sts.

Rows 1-2: Knit.

Row 3 (inc): Kfb, k3[5], kfb (7[9] sts).

Row 4: Knit.

Row 5 (inc): Kfb, k5[7], kfb (9[11] sts).

Rows 6-10: Knit.

Adult size only

Knit 4 rows.

Both sizes

Next row (dec): K2tog, k5[7], k2tog (7[9] sts).

Next row: Knit.

Next row (dec): K2tog, k3[5], k2tog (5[7] sts).

Next 2 rows: Knit.

Cast off.

MAKING UP

Using matching yarn, join the back seam of main section.

Position the wrong side of ears over right side of facings and hat. Slipstitch in place, leaving the buttonholes free.

Sew eye patch to front of main section. Stitch side edges of nose together and, folding the piece with the seam at centre back, join the lower narrow cast-on edge, then the wider cast-off edge. Attach the nose to the centre front of the hat, just above the garter-stitch edge.

Using sewing thread, sew a cream button to each of the tops of the ears. Place the black buttons over the remaining cream buttons and stitch to the main section for the eyes.

LINING THE HAT

See pages 104–109 for how to make and attach a cosy fleece or knitted lining for your hat.

koala

This cuddly koala with its snuggly embrace and
bobble ears gives a sense of the furry creature atop a
eucalyptus tree. Long pompom-tipped ties add length
and height as the bear clings to its holding place.

MATERIALS
Wendy Merino Chunky, 100% merino wool
    (71yds/65m per 50g ball)
3[3] x 50g balls in 2472 Pumice (A)
1[1] x 50g ball in 2470 Cloud (B)
Wendy Merino Bliss DK, 100% merino wool
    (126yds/116m per 50g ball)
1[1] x 50g ball in 2366 Jet (C)
1 pair each of 7mm (UK2:US10.5/11) and
    4mm (UK8:US6) needles
2 x brown ¾[⅞]in (2[2.25]cm) diameter buttons
2 x black ½[⅝]in (1.25[1.5]cm) diameter buttons
Small amount of toy stuffing
Stitch holder
Darning needle
Sewing needle
Black sewing thread
Thin card to make pompoms

SIZES
To fit: child up to 8 years [adult]

TENSION
13 sts and 18 rows to 4in (10cm) over stocking
stitch using 7mm needles. Use larger or smaller
needles if necessary to obtain correct tension.

METHOD

The triangular shaped earflaps are worked first and joined at the lower edge of the crown of the hat. Ear facings are knitted to line the earflaps. Pompoms form the koala's ears, with another pair decorating the ends of the twisted cords that are attached to the tips of the earflaps. A large, stuffed nose finishes the bear, along with button eyes.

MAIN PIECE

First earflap

Both sizes

*Using 7mm needles and A, cast on 3 sts.
Row 1 (inc) (RS): Kfb, k1, kfb (5 sts).
Row 2: K2, p1, k2.
Row 3 (inc): Kfb, k3, kfb (7 sts).
Row 4: K2, p3, k2.
Row 5 (inc): Kfb, k5, kfb (9 sts).

Row 6: K2, p5, k2.
Row 7 (inc): Kfb, k7, kfb (11 sts).
Row 8: K2, p7, k2.
Row 9 (inc): Kfb, k9, kfb (13 sts).
Row 10: K2, p9, k2.
Row 11 (inc): Kfb, k11, kfb (15 sts).
Row 12: K2, p11, k2.

Adult size only

Row 13 (inc): Kfb, k13, kfb (17 sts).
Row 14: K2, p13, k2.

Both sizes

Row 15: Knit.
Row 16: As row 12[14].*
Break yarn and leave these sts on a holder.

Second earflap

Work as given for first earflap from * to *.
Next row: Cast on and k 5 sts, knit across 15[17] sts of second earflap, turn, cast on

21 sts, turn, knit across 15[17] sts of first earflap, turn, cast on 5 sts (61[65] sts).
Next row (WS): K7, p11[13], k25, p11[13], k7.
Next row: Knit.
Rep last 2 rows once more and then, starting with a p row, work 19[21] rows in st st, ending with a WS row.

Shape crown

Row 1 (RS) (dec): K2tog, (k12[13], sl1, k2tog, psso) 3 times, k12[13], k2tog (53[57] sts).
Row 2: Purl.
Row 3 (dec): K2tog, (k10[11], sl1, k2tog, psso) 3 times, k10[11], k2tog (45[49] sts).
Row 4: Purl.
Row 5 (dec): K2tog, (k8[9], sl1, k2tog, psso) 3 times, k8[9], k2tog (37[41] sts).
Row 6: Purl.

Row 7 (dec): K2tog, (k6[7], sl1, k2tog, psso) 3 times, k6[7], k2tog (29[33] sts).
Row 8: Purl.
Row 9 (dec): K2tog, (k4[5], sl1, k2tog, psso) 3 times, k4[5], k2tog (21[25] sts).
Row 10: Purl.
Row 11 (dec): K2tog, (k2[3], sl1, k2tog, psso) 3 times, k2[3], k2tog (13[17] sts).
Adult size only
Row 12: Purl.
Row 13 (dec): K2tog, (k1, sl1, k2tog, psso) 3 times, k1, k2tog (9 sts).
Both sizes
Break yarn and thread through rem sts, draw up tight and fasten off.

EARFLAP FACING (MAKE 2)
Omit if you plan to add knitted lining
Using 7mm needles and A, cast on 3 sts and work rows 1–16 of pattern for earflaps.
Next: Rep rows 15 and 16 three more times. Cast off loosely.

NOSE
Using 4mm needles and C, cast on 18[21] sts.
Beg with a k row, work 1⅝[2]in (4[5]cm) in st st, ending with a p row.
Shape top
Next row (RS) (dec): (K1, k2tog) 6[7] times (12[14] sts).
Next row: Purl.
Next row (dec): (k2tog) 6[7] times (6[7] sts).
Next row: Purl.
Break yarn and thread through rem sts, gather up and fasten off.

MAKING UP
Using matching yarn, join the back seam.

With right sides together, sew the earflap facings to the earflaps, starting and finishing at the edge of the main section, leaving the overlapping cast-on edge open. Turn right side out and slipstitch the open edges to the inside of the main section.

Join seam of the nose and stuff the piece lightly. With the seam at the centre back of the work, slipstitch the cast-on edge together to join. Attach the nose to the main part of the hat at the centre front, just above the garter-stitch border. Using B, make two pompom ears (see page 118) measuring 2⅜[3]in (6[7.5]cm) across. Stitch to each side of the hat at the beginning of shaping. Make two twisted cords using A (see page 118), each measuring 8[12]in (20[30] cm) long, using 6[8] strands of yarn. Make two 2[2⅜]in (5[6]cm) pompoms in A and attach each to one end of the twisted cord, then stitch the other end of the cord to the tip of the earflap.

Using sewing thread, place the small black buttons over the larger brown buttons and sew in place for the eyes.

LINING THE HAT
See pages 104–109 for how to make and attach a cosy fleece or knitted lining.

panda

A cuddly creature in striking monochrome, this cute
panda bear is easy to knit in chunky yarn, his distinct
features making him an instantly recognisable,
warm addition to your winter wardrobe.

MATERIALS

Wendy Mode Chunky, 50% pure merino wool, 50%
    fine acrylic (153yds/140m per 100g ball)
1[1] x 100g balls in 201 Whisper White (A)
1[1] x 100g ball in 220 Coal (B)
1 pair of 7mm (UK2:US10.5/11) needles
2 x white ¾[⅞]in (2[2.25]cm) diameter buttons
2 x black ½[⅝]in (1.25[1.5]cm) diameter buttons
Small amount of toy stuffing
Stitch holder
Darning needle
Sewing needle
Black sewing thread
Thin card to make pompoms

SIZES

To fit: child up to 8 years [adult]

TENSION

13 sts and 18 rows to 4in (10cm) over stocking
stitch using 7mm needles. Use larger or smaller
needles if necessary to obtain correct tension.

METHOD

The main part of the hat is decorated with eye patches, large, round ears and a nose knitted separately. The button eyes finish off the features. Pompoms are attached to twisted cords, which hang from each earflap.

MAIN PIECE

First earflap

Both sizes

*Using 7mm needles and A, cast on 3 sts.

Row 1 (inc) (RS): Kfb, k1, kfb (5 sts).

Row 2: K2, p1, k2.

Row 3 (inc): Kfb, k3, kfb (7 sts).

Row 4: K2, p3, k2.

Row 5 (inc): Kfb, k5, kfb (9 sts).

Row 6: K2, p5, k2.

Row 7 (inc): Kfb, k7, kfb (11 sts).

Row 8: K2, p7, k2.

Row 9 (inc): Kfb, k9, kfb (13 sts).

Row 10: K2, p9, k2.

Row 11 (inc): Kfb, k11, kfb (15 sts).

Row 12: K2, p11, k2.

Adult size only

Row 13 (inc): Kfb, k13, kfb (17 sts).

Row 14: K2, p13, k2.

Both sizes

Row 15: Knit.

Row 16: As row 12[14].*

Break yarn and leave these sts on a holder.

Second earflap

Work as given for first earflap from * to *.

Next row: Cast on and k 5 sts, knit across 15[17] sts of second earflap, turn, cast on 21 sts, turn, knit across 15[17] sts of first earflap, turn, cast on 5 sts (61[65] sts).

Next row (WS): K7, p11[13], k25, p11[13], k7.

Next row: Knit.

Rep last 2 rows once more and then starting with a p row, work 19[21] rows in st st, ending with a WS row.

Shape crown

Row 1 (RS) (dec): K2tog, (k12[13], sl1, k2tog, psso) 3 times, k12[13], k2tog (53[57] sts).

Row 2: Purl.

Row 3 (dec): K2tog, (k10[11], sl1, k2tog, psso) 3 times, k10[11], k2tog (45[49] sts).

Row 4: Purl.

Row 5 (dec): K2tog, (k8[9], sl1, k2tog, psso) 3 times, k8[9], k2tog (37[41] sts).

Row 6: Purl.

Row 7 (dec): K2tog, (k6[7], sl1, k2tog, psso) 3 times, k6[7], k2tog (29[33] sts).

Row 8: Purl.

Row 9 (dec): K2tog, (k4[5], sl1, k2tog, psso) 3 times, k4[5], k2tog (21[25] sts).

Row 10: Purl.

Row 11 (dec): K2tog, (k2[3], sl1, k2tog, psso) 3 times, k2[3], k2tog (13[17] sts).

Adult size only

Row 12: Purl.

Row 13 (dec): K2tog, (k1, sl1, k2tog, psso) 3 times, k1, k2tog (9 sts).

Both sizes

Break yarn and thread through rem sts, draw up tight and fasten off.

EARFLAP FACING (MAKE 2)

Omit if you plan to add knitted lining

Using 7mm needles and A, cast on 3 sts and work rows 1 to 16 of pattern for earflaps.

Next: Rep rows 15 and 16 three more times.

Cast off loosely.

EYE PATCHES (MAKE 2)

Both sizes

Using 7mm needles and B, cast on 5 sts.

Rows 1–2: Knit.

Row 3 (inc): Kfb, k3, kfb (7 sts).

Adult size only

Row 4: Knit.

Row 5 (inc): Kfb, k5, kfb (9 sts).

Both sizes

Rows 6–12: Knit.

Adult size only

Rows 13–16: Knit.

Row 17 (dec): K2tog, k5, k2tog (7 sts).

Row 18: Knit.

Both sizes

Row 19 (dec): K2tog, k3, k2tog (5 sts).

Rows 20–21: Knit.

Cast off.

EARS (MAKE 2)

Using 7mm needles and B, cast on 7[9] sts.

Rows 1–2: Knit.

Row 3 (inc): Kfb, k5[7], kfb (9[11] sts).

Adult size only

Row 4: Knit.

Row 5 (inc): Kfb, k9, kfb (13 sts).

Both sizes

Rows 6–10: Knit.

Adult size only

Rows 11–12: Knit.

Row 13 (dec): K2tog, k9, k2tog (11 sts).

Row 14: Knit.

Both sizes

Row 15 (dec): K2tog, k5[7], k2tog (7[9] sts).

Row 16: Knit.

Row 17 (dec): K2tog, k3[5], k2tog (5[7] sts).

Rows 18: Knit.

Row 19 (inc): Kfb, k3[5], kfb (7[9] sts).

Rows 20–36: As rows 2–16.

Knit 1 row.

Cast off.

NOSE

Both sizes

Starting at the narrow base of the nose, with 7mm needles and yarn B, cast on 3 sts.

Row 1 (RS): Knit.

Row 2: Purl.

Row 3 (inc): (Kfb) 3 times (6 sts).

Row 4: Purl.

Adult size only

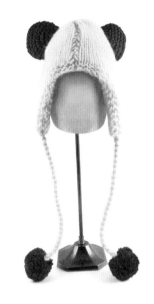

Row 5 (inc): (Kfb) 6 times (12 sts).

Row 6: Purl.

Row 7 (dec): (K2tog) 6 times (6 sts).

Row 8: Purl.

Both sizes

Row 9 (dec): (K2tog) 3 times (3 sts).

Row 10: Purl.

Row 11: Knit.

Cast off knitwise.

MAKING UP

Using matching yarn, join the back seam.

With right sides together, sew the earflap facings to the earflaps, starting and finishing at the edge of the main section, leaving the overlapping cast-on edge open. Turn right side out and slipstitch the open edges to the inside of the main section.

Fold nose with wrong sides together, matching the cast-on and cast-off edges. Join the seams neatly. Attach the nose to the centre front of the hat, with the narrow end sitting just above the garter-stitch edge.

Fold ear with right sides together and join the shaped side seams, leaving the cast-on and cast-off edges open. Turn right side out, stuff lightly then close the seam. Fold the lower edge, bringing each corner to the centre to shape the ear and stitch in place. Attach the ears to each side of the hat at around one third from the beginning of the shaping.

Make two twisted cords using A (see page 118), each measuring 8[12]in (20[30]cm) long, using 6[8] strands of yarn. Make two 2[2⅜]in (5[6]cm) pompoms in B (see page 118) and attach each to one end of the twisted cord, then stitch the other end of the cord to the tip of the earflap.

Using sewing thread, place the small black buttons over the larger white buttons and sew onto the panda's patches for the eyes.

LINING THE HAT

See pages 104–109 for how to make and attach a cosy fleece or knitted lining for your hat.

COW

The markings on this hat can be placed anywhere to make your Friesian unique. You can easily create another breed of cow, such as a Jersey, by substituting the cream and black for a shade of light brown.

MATERIALS

Debbie Bliss Rialto Chunky, 100% merino wool
(65yds/60m per 50g ball)

3[3] x 50g balls in 003 Ecru (A)

1[2] x 50g balls in 006 Camel (B)

2[2] x 50g balls in 001 Black (C)

1 pair of 7mm (UK2:US10.5/11) needles

2 x brown $7/8$[$1\frac{1}{8}$]in (2.25[2.75]cm) diameter
buttons

4 x black $\frac{1}{2}$[$5/8$]in (1.25[1.5]cm) diameter buttons

Small amount of toy stuffing

Stitch holder

Darning needle

Sewing needle

Black sewing thread

Thin card to make tassels

SIZES

To fit: child up to 8 years [adult]

TENSION

13 sts and 18 rows to 4in (10cm) over stocking
stitch using 7mm needles. Use larger or smaller
needles if necessary to obtain correct tension.

METHOD

After making up the main part of the hat in stocking stitch, the features that create the finished look are knitted and attached. The ears are knitted in two pieces and sewn together, bringing the corners of the lower edges to meet in the centre to form the shape. The curved horns are created by increasing and decreasing stitches. The garter-stitch patches are positioned randomly over the hat.

MAIN PIECE

First earflap
Both sizes
*Using 7mm needles and A, cast on 3 sts.
Row 1 (inc) (RS): Kfb, k1, kfb (5 sts).
Row 2: K2, p1, k2.
Row 3 (inc): Kfb, k3, kfb (7 sts).
Row 4: K2, p3, k2.
Row 5 (inc): Kfb, k5, kfb (9 sts).
Row 6: K2, p5, k2.
Row 7 (inc): Kfb, k7, kfb (11 sts).
Row 8: K2, p7, k2.
Row 9 (inc): Kfb, k9, kfb (13 sts).
Row 10: K2, p9, k2.
Row 11 (inc): Kfb, k11, kfb (15 sts).
Row 12: K2, p11, k2.
Adult size only
Row 13 (inc): Kfb, k13, kfb (17 sts).
Row 14: K2, p13, k2.
Both sizes
Row 15: Knit.
Row 16: As row 12[14].*
Break yarn and leave these sts on a holder.

Second earflap
Work as given for first earflap from * to *.
Next row: Cast on and k 5 sts, knit across 15[17] sts of second earflap, turn, cast on 21 sts, turn, knit across 15[17] sts of first earflap, turn, cast on 5 sts (61[65] sts).
Next row (WS): K7, p11[13], k25, p11[13], k7.
Next row: Knit.
Rep last 2 rows once more and then starting with a purl row, work 19[21] rows in st st, ending with a WS row.
Shape crown
Row 1 (RS) (dec): K2tog, (k12[13], sl1, k2tog, psso) 3 times, k12[13], k2tog (53[57] sts).
Row 2: Purl.
Row 3 (dec): K2tog, (k10[11], sl1, k2tog, psso) 3 times, k10[11], k2tog (45[49] sts).
Row 4: Purl.
Row 5 (dec): K2tog, (k8[9], sl1, k2tog, psso) 3 times, k8[9], k2tog (37[41] sts).
Row 6: Purl.
Row 7 (dec): K2tog, (k6[7], sl1, k2tog, psso) 3 times, k6[7], k2tog (29[33] sts).
Row 8: Purl.
Row 9 (dec): K2tog, (k4[5], sl1, k2tog, psso) 3 times, k4[5], k2tog (21[25] sts).
Row 10: Purl.
Row 11 (dec): K2tog, (k2[3], sl1, k2tog, psso) 3 times, k2[3], k2tog (13[17] sts).
Adult size only
Row 12: Purl.
Row 13 (dec): K2tog, (k1, sl1, k2tog, psso) 3 times, k1, k2tog (9 sts).

Both sizes
Break yarn and thread through rem sts, draw up tight and fasten off.

EARFLAP FACING (MAKE 2)

Omit if you plan to add knitted lining
Using 7mm needles and A, cast on 3 sts and work as for earflaps.
Next: Rep rows 15 and 16 three more times.
Cast off loosely.

OUTER EAR (MAKE 2)

Both sizes
With 7mm needles and C, cast on 3 sts.
Row 1 (inc): Kfb, k1, kfb (5 sts).
Row 2: Purl.
Row 3 (inc): Kfb, k3, kfb (7 sts).
Row 4: Purl.
Row 5 (inc): Kfb, k5, kfb (9 sts).
Row 6: Purl.
Row 7 (inc): Kfb, k7, kfb (11 sts).
Row 8: Purl.
Row 9 (inc): Kfb, k9, kfb (13 sts).
Adult size only
Row 10: Purl.
Row 11 (inc): Kfb, k11, kfb (15 sts).
Both sizes
Work 9 rows in st st.
Cast off.

INNER EAR (MAKE 2)

Both sizes
With 7mm needles and C, cast on 3 sts.
Work as given for outer ear.

NOSE
With 7mm needles and B, cast on 15[17] sts.
Work 8[10] rows in g-st.
Next row (WS) (dec): K2tog, k11[13], k2tog (13[15] sts).
Next row: Knit.
Next row (dec): K2tog, k9[11] k2tog (11[13] sts).
Next row: Knit.
Next row (dec): K2tog, k7[9], k2tog (9[11] sts).
Cast off.

PATCHES (MAKE 4)
Both sizes
With 7mm needles and C, cast on 5 sts.
Row 1 (inc): Kfb, k3, kfb (7 sts).
Row 2: Knit.
Row 3 (inc): Kfb, k5, kfb (9 sts).
Adult size only
Row 4: Knit.
Row 5 (inc): Kfb, k7, kfb (11 sts).
Both sizes
Knit 5[7] rows.
Next row (dec): K2tog, k5[7], k2tog (7[9] sts).
Next row: Knit.
Next row (dec): K2tog, k3[5], k2tog (5[7] sts).
Knit 6 rows.
Next row (dec): K2tog, k1[3], k2tog (3[5] sts). Cast off.

HORNS (MAKE 2)
With 7mm needles and B DOUBLED, cast on 11[15] sts.

Row 1 (dec): K2tog, k to last 2 sts, k2tog (9[13] sts).
Row 2: Purl.
Adult size only
Row 3 (dec): K2tog, k to last 2 sts, k2tog (11 sts).
Row 4: Purl.
Both sizes
Row 5: Kfb, k2[3], sl1, k2tog, psso, k2[3], kfb.
Row 6: Purl.
Rep rows 5 and 6 once[twice] more.
Next row (dec): K3[4], sl1, k2tog, psso, k3[4] (7[9] sts).
Next row: Purl.
Next row (dec): K2tog, k0[1], sl 1, k2tog, psso, k0[1], k2tog (3[5] sts).
Break yarn and thread through rem sts. Fasten off.

MAKING UP
Using matching yarn, join the back seam.

With right sides together, sew the earflap facings to the earflaps, starting and finishing at the edge of the main section, leaving the overlapping cast-on edge open. Turn right side out and slipstitch the open edges to the inside of the main section.

Join the curved seam of the horns. Stuff firmly and attach to the top of the hat, curving in towards each other. With right sides together join the two ear pieces, leaving the lower edge open. Turn right sides out and join the cast-off edges.

Bring the two corners of each side from the lower edge of the ear to the middle to form a bowl shape. Stitch to hold in place. Attach to the main section of the hat, next to each horn, stitching all around the lower shaped ear.

Stitch the nose in place on the front of the hat with the cast-on edge sitting just above the rows of garter stitch, leaving an opening. Stuff lightly to create some shape. Close the opening and fasten off neatly.

Sew the patches in place to the main section, positioning them around the front and back of the hat.

Make two twisted cords using A (see page 118), each measuring 8[12]in (20[30]cm), using 6[8] strands of yarn. Make two tassels (see page 119) measuring 4[5⅛]in (10[13]cm) long in C, and attach each to one end of the twisted cord, then stitch the other end of the cord to the tip of the earflap.

Using sewing thread, place the small black buttons over the larger brown buttons and sew in place for the eyes. Sew the remaining small black buttons in place for the nostrils.

LINING THE HAT
See pages 104–109 for how to make and attach a cosy fleece or knitted lining for your hat.

lining your hat

sewing in a
fleece lining

This lining can be added to all of the hats in this book
to make them even cosier. Polar fleece is recommended,
but jersey or towelling fabrics can also be used.

MATERIALS

22 x 22in (56 x 56cm)
[25 x 25in (63.5 x 63.5cm)]
   polar fleece fabric
Matching thread
Needle
Dressmaking pins
³⁄₈in (1cm) squared pattern paper
   (or access to a photocopier)
Pencil
Scissors

METHOD

1 Using the pattern templates on page 106, scale them to the size that you require (adult- or child-sized), either by transferring onto squared pattern paper (or by photocopying at 200%).

2 Cut out the paper pattern following the unbroken lines. Seam allowances of ⁵⁄₈in (1.5cm) are included in the pattern with the stitches indicated as a broken line inside the continuous black outline.

3 Fold the fabric at a 45-degree angle to obtain the bias. This is the diagonal line that cuts across the warp and the weft, or the vertical and horizontal threads of the fabric (see drawing opposite).

4 Place the pattern on the folded fleece so the arrow of the grain line on the paper follows the direction of the vertical threads of the fabric to allow some elasticity in the finished lining. Ensure the fold indicated on the pattern is placed exactly on the bias fold of the fabric. Pin the pattern in position and cut out the fleece.

5 Stitch the darts where indicated on the pattern template. Pin the main seam along the broken line and stitch together. Cut notches into the curved edge (see opposite) and trim the seam.

6 Turn under a hem of ⁵⁄₈in (1.5cm) and pin the lining to the inside of the finished hat, just above the cast-on stitches, with the main seam matching the back seam of the hat. Ease the fabric evenly around the lower edge. Slipstitch the fleece lining in place by hand. Put a few stitches through the top of the crown into the knitted hat to keep it in place.

FINDING THE BIAS

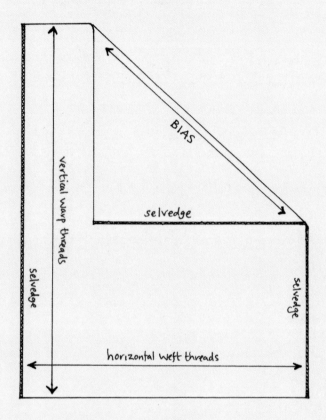

BIAS

selvedge

vertical warp threads

selvedge

selvedge

horizontal weft threads

CUTTING NOTCHES

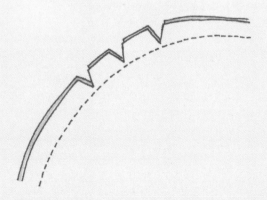

PATTERN TEMPLATE
1 square = ⅜ in (1cm)

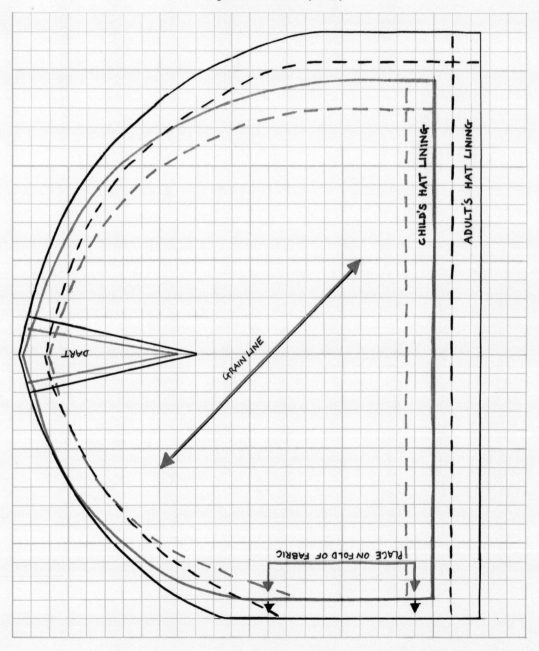

DART

GRAIN LINE

CHILD'S HAT LINING

ADULT'S HAT LINING

PLACE ON FOLD OF FABRIC

Enlarge by 200% on a photocopier. ▸Align marker with arrow on top left of photocopier glass.

inserting a knitted lining

A knitted lining is a cosy alternative to using fleece.
It can either be worked in the same shade as your
animal hat or in a contrasting colour.

MATERIALS

100g of yarn used
  for chosen animal hat (A)
Please see chosen animal hat
  pattern for needle sizes required
Stitch holder
Darning needle

SIZE
To fit: child up to 8 years [adult]

TENSION
See chosen animal hat pattern
for required tension

METHOD

The knitted lining is worked in the same
yarn as the animal you are making, so
refer to the pattern for the yarn type,
needles required and tension. The earflap
facings are worked first, where applicable,
and then the main part of the lining is
continued in stocking stitch. The back
seam is joined and the lining slipped
inside the hat and stitched in place before
finishing with twisted cords and tassels
or pompoms, if using.

PATTERN NOTE

As the earflap facings are worked into
the knitted lining pattern, omit them
where applicable from the main animal
pattern when knitting the outer section
of the hat, apart from those of the Dog
and Penguin. The lining is stitched in place
after the features are added to the main
part of the hat. If twisted cords are to
be attached to the earflaps, the knitted
lining should go in first.

KNITTED LINING FOR RABBIT, CHICKEN, COW, ELEPHANT, FOX, KOALA, MONKEY, MOUSE AND PANDA

First earflap facing

Both sizes

*Using 6mm needles for Monkey, 6.5mm needles for Rabbit and 7mm needles for Chicken, Cow, Elephant, Fox, Koala, Mouse and Panda, and A, cast on 3 sts.

Row 1 (inc) (RS): Kfb, k1, kfb (5 sts).
Row 2: K2, p1, k2.
Row 3 (inc): Kfb, k3, kfb (7 sts).
Row 4: K2, p3, k2.
Row 5 (inc): Kfb, k5, kfb (9 sts).
Row 6: K2, p5, k2.
Row 7 (inc): Kfb, k7, kfb (11 sts).
Row 8: K2, p7, k2.
Row 9 (inc): Kfb, k9, kfb (13 sts).
Row 10: K2, p9, k2.
Row 11 (inc): Kfb, k11, kfb (15 sts).
Row 12: K2, p11, k2.

Adult size only

Row 13 (inc): Kfb, k13, kfb (17 sts).
Row 14: K2, p13, k2.

Both sizes

Row 15: Knit.
Row 16: As row 12[14].*
Break yarn and leave sts on a holder.

Second earflap facing

Work as given for first earflap from * to *.
Next row: Cast on and k 5 sts, knit across 15[17] sts of second earflap, turn, cast on 21 sts, turn, knit across 15[17] sts of first earflap, turn, cast on 5 sts (61[65] sts).
Next row (WS): K7, p11[13], k25, p11[13], k7.
Next row: Knit.
Rep last 2 rows once more and then starting with a p row, work 19[21] rows in st st, ending with a WS row.

Shape crown

Row 1 (RS) (dec): K2tog, (k12[13], sl1, k2tog, psso) 3 times, k12[13], k2tog (53[57] sts).
Row 2: Purl.
Row 3 (dec): K2tog, (k10[11], sl1, k2tog, psso) 3 times, k10[11], k2tog (45[49] sts).
Row 4: Purl.
Row 5 (dec): K2tog, (k8[9], sl1, k2tog, psso) 3 times, k8[9], k2tog (37[41] sts).
Row 6: Purl.
Row 7 (dec): K2tog, (k6[7], sl1, k2tog, psso) 3 times, k6[7], k2tog (29[33] sts).
Row 8: Purl.
Row 9 (dec): K2tog, (k4[5], sl1, k2tog, psso) 3 times, k4[5], k2tog (21[25] sts).
Row 10: Purl.
Row 11 (dec): K2tog, (k2[3], sl1, k2tog, psso) 3 times, k2[3], k2tog (13[17] sts).

Adult size only

Row 12: Purl.
Row 13 (dec): K2tog, (k1, sl1, k2tog, psso) 3 times, k1, k2tog (9 sts).

Both sizes

Break yarn and thread through rem sts, draw up tight and fasten off.

KNITTED LINING FOR PIG

With 7mm needles and A, cast on 61[65] sts.
Starting with a knit row, work in st st for 16[18] rows, ending with a WS row.

Shape crown

Work as for Rabbit, Chicken, Cow, Elephant, Fox, Koala, Monkey, Mouse and Panda.

KNITTED LINING FOR DOG AND PENGUIN

With 7mm needles and A, cast on 61[65] sts.
Work 3 rows in g-st.
Starting with a knit row, work in st st for 20[22] rows, ending with a WS row.

Shape crown

Row 1 (RS) (dec): K2tog, k11[12], sl1, k2tog, psso, (k13[14], sl1, k2tog, psso) twice, k11[12], k2tog (53[57] sts).
Row 2: Purl.
Row 3 (dec): K2tog, k9[10], sl1, k2tog, psso, (k11[12], sl1, k2tog, psso) twice, k9[10], k2tog (45[49] sts).
Row 4: Purl.
Row 5 (dec): K2tog, k7[8], sl1, k2tog, psso, (k9[10], sl1, k2tog, psso) twice, k9[8], k2tog (37[41] sts).
Row 6: Purl.
Row 7 (dec): K2tog, k5[6], sl1, k2tog, psso, (k7[8], sl1, k2tog, psso) twice, k5[6], k2tog (29[33] sts).
Row 8: Purl.
Row 9 (dec): K2tog, k3[4], sl1, k2tog, psso, (k5[6], sl1, k2tog, psso) twice, k3[4], k2tog (21[25] sts).
Row 10: Purl.
Row 11 (dec): K2tog, k1[2], sl1, k2tog, psso, (k3[4], sl1, k2tog, psso) twice, k1[2], k2tog (13[17] sts).

Adult size only

Row 12: Purl.
Row 13 (dec): K2tog, sl1, k2tog, psso, (k2, sl1, k2tog, psso) twice, k2tog (9 sts).

Both sizes

Break yarn and thread through rem sts, draw up tight and fasten off.

KNITTED LINING FOR FROG AND LION

First earflap facing

Both sizes

*With 10mm needles for Frog and 12mm needles for Lion and A, cast on 3 sts.

Row 1 (inc) (RS): Kfb, k1, kfb (5 sts).
Row 2: K2, p1, k2.
Row 3 (inc): Kfb, k3, kfb (7 sts).
Row 4: K2, p3, k2.
Row 5 (inc): Kfb, k5, kfb (9 sts).
Row 6: K2, p5, k2.

Adult size only

Row 7 (inc): Kfb, k7, kfb (11 sts).
Row 8: K2, p7, k2.

Both sizes

Row 9: Knit.
Row 10: As row 6 [8].*
Break yarn and leave these sts on a holder.

Second earflap facing

Work as given for first earflap from * to *.
Next row: Cast on and k 4 sts, knit across 9[11] sts of second earflap, turn, cast on 15 sts, turn, knit across 9[11] sts of first earflap, turn, cast on 4 sts (41[45] sts).
Next row (WS): K6, p5[7], k19, p5[7], k6.
Next row (RS): Knit.
Rep first of last 2 rows once more.
Starting with a knit row, work 16 rows in stocking stitch, ending with a purl row.

Shape crown

Row 1 (dec) (RS): K2tog, (k7[8], sl1, k2tog, psso) 3 times, k7[8], k2tog (33[37] sts).
Row 2: Purl.
Row 3 (dec): K2tog, (k5[6], sl1, k2tog, psso) 3 times, k5[6], k2tog (25[29] sts).
Row 4: Purl.
Row 5 (dec): K2tog, (k3[4], sl1, k2tog, psso) 3 times, k3[4], k2tog (17[21] sts).
Row 6: Purl.
Row 7 (dec): K2tog, (k1[2], sl1, k2tog, psso) 3 times, k1[2], k2tog (9[13] sts).
Break yarn and thread through rem sts, draw up tight and fasten off.

KNITTED LINING FOR CAT

With 7.5mm needles and A, cast on 41[45] sts.
Work 3 rows in g-st.
Change to 8mm needles.
Starting with a k row, work 14[16] rows in st st.

Shape crown

Work as for Frog and Lion.

MAKING UP

Using matching yarn, join the back seam. With wrong sides together, pin the lining in place inside the main part of the hat and slipstitch neatly around the lower edges. For the Dog and Penguin, pin in position matching lower edges and keeping the lining straight across the earflap facings before stitching. For the Pig, slipstitch the lower edge of the lining to the first row of stocking stitch after the rib on the main part. Work a few stitches into the top of the crown to stop the lining slipping.

basic techniques

getting started

When starting a new project, always read the materials list at the beginning of the pattern carefully to see what you will need to gather together.

SIZING

The finished animal hats are intended to fit children up to 8 years of age and adults. They should fit an average size head. See 'Reading patterns'.

TENSION

Checking the tension before starting a project is vital as this will affect the size and look of the finished piece. The tension is the number of rows and stitches per square inch or centimetre of knitted fabric. A knitted sample should be big enough to enable you to measure easily – around 5in (13cm) square.

Using the same needles and stitch that the tension has been measured over in the pattern, knit a sample then smooth out on a flat surface. Place a ruler across the work horizontally and mark 4in (10cm) with pins. Count the number of stitches between the pins, including half stitches. This will give you the tension of stitches.

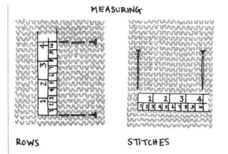

MEASURING

ROWS   STITCHES

Measure the tension of rows by placing a ruler vertically over the work and mark 4in (10cm) with pins. Count the number of rows between the pins. If the numbers are greater than those stated in the pattern, your tension is tighter and you should use larger needles. If the number of stitches and rows is less than those stated in the pattern, your tension is looser, so you should use smaller needles.

SUBSTITUTING YARNS

When substituting yarns, it is important to calculate the number of balls required by the number of yards or metres per ball rather than the weight of the yarn, as this varies according to the fibre. Tension is also important. Work a tension swatch in the yarn you wish to use before starting a project.

READING PATTERNS

The animal hat patterns are written for both children's and adults' sizes. The children's size is given first and where the adults' instructions differ, the adjustment is given inside square [ ] brackets. If 0 appears in the instructions, then no stitches or rows are to be worked for this size. Where there is no bracket after the stitches or rows given, the instructions refer to both of the sizes.

READING CHARTS

Each square of a chart represents one stitch and each horizontal row represents one row of knitting. The changes of colour or pattern are shown as actual colour or symbols. Read the chart from the bottom row to the top, working from right to left for the right-side rows and from left to right for wrong-side rows.

knitting basics

Here, all the knitting basics you will need are clearly explained, from casting on and off to sewing up the seams and making pompoms.

SLIP KNOT

The first stitch on the needle is the slip knot or slip loop.

1 Take the end of the yarn and form it into a ring. Insert the needle through the ring, catching the long end that is attached to the ball, and draw it back through.

2 Keeping the yarn looped on the needle, pull through until the loop closes around the needle, ensuring it is not tight. Pulling on the short end of yarn will loosen the knot, whilst the long end will tighten it.

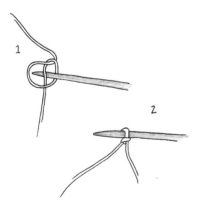

CABLE CAST ON

This produces a corded foundation row, suitable for items that require an elastic but firm edge.

1 With the slip knot on the left-hand needle, insert the right-hand needle and pass the yarn under and over the point.

2 Pull this loop just made through the stitch.

3 Pass the loop onto the left-hand needle.

4 For the third and following stitches, insert the right-hand needle between the two stitches on the left-hand needle; pass the yarn around the point of the right-hand needle to make a loop and pull through to the front of the work. Pass the loop onto the left-hand needle.

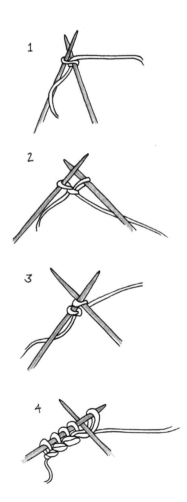

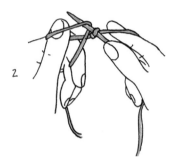

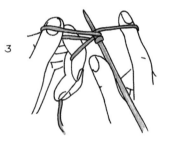

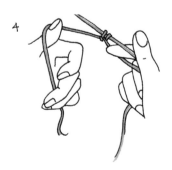

THUMB METHOD

This edge is worked towards the end of the yarn rather than the ball, as in the previous methods, so allow enough length at the beginning.

1 Make a slip knot, leaving a long length of yarn. Hold the needle in the right hand and with the length of yarn in the left, pass it around the left thumb and hold in place with the fingers.

2 Insert the needle under and up through the loop on the thumb.

3 With the right hand, pass the yarn from the ball up and over the point of the needle.

4 Draw the yarn through the loop on the thumb, forming the new stitch on the needle. Remove the thumb from the loop and pull on the end of the yarn to tighten the stitch.

KNIT STITCH

This stitch creates a reversible fabric of garter stitch when worked on every row. Each stitch is worked from the left-hand needle to the right-hand needle to form a row of knitting. Then the needles are swapped to the opposite hands to begin another row.

1 Insert the right-hand needle through the first stitch on the left-hand needle, from front to back.

2 Pass the yarn around the point of the right-hand needle.

3 Draw the loop through the stitch, thus forming the new stitch on the right-hand needle.

4 Slip the original stitch off the left-hand needle at the same time. Continue in this way for each stitch.

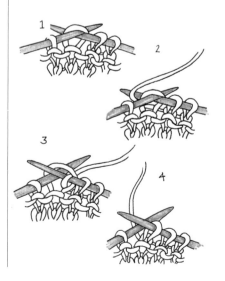

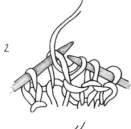

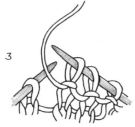

PURL STITCH

The purl stitch is the reverse of the knit stitch. The stitch on the left-hand needle is slipped off to the front of the work. If the purl stitch is used on every row, the effect will be the same as the knit stitch, creating a garter-stitch fabric. By alternating rows of knit and purl, the stocking-stitch fabric is produced. A rib is formed by alternating knit and purl stitches.

1 With the yarn at the front of the work, insert the right-hand needle through the first stitch, from back to front. Pass the yarn in an anti-clockwise direction around the point of the right-hand needle.

2 Draw the loop through the stitch, forming the new stitch on the right-hand needle.

3 Slip the original stitch off the left-hand needle at the same time. Continue in this way for each stitch.

GARTER STITCH

Knit every row.

STOCKING STITCH

Row 1 (RS): Knit.
Row 2 (WS): Purl.
Repeat rows 1 and 2 to form the stocking stitch.

REVERSE STOCKING STITCH

This is the reverse side of the stocking stitch, where the purl rows are on the right side of the fabric.
Row 1 (RS): Purl.
Row 2 (WS): Knit.
Repeat rows 1 and 2 to form the reverse stocking stitch.

GARTER STITCH

STOCKING STITCH

REVERSE STOCKING STITCH

LOOP STITCH

In steps 1 and 2, the yarn is wound in a figure-of-eight direction to create two loops on the right-hand needle. The yarn that has been wound around the finger will create the finished loop of the mane.

1 Insert the right-hand needle into next stitch, with left forefinger behind the right-hand needle. Wind yarn in a clockwise direction over the right-hand needle and forefinger once.

2 Then wind yarn around the right-hand needle as usual, in an anticlockwise direction, knit the stitch, keeping the forefinger in the loop.

3 Slip both loops just made back onto the left-hand needle and knit them together through the back loops.

4 Remove the finger from the loop. Pull the loop to the front of the work before commencing with the next stitch.

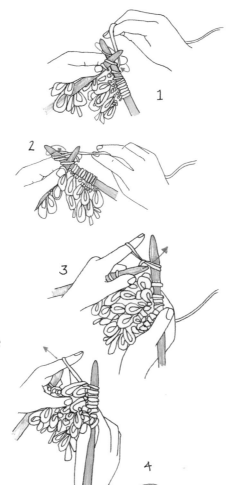

CASTING OFF

Casting off keeps the stitches from unravelling and creates a neat edge. It is important not to cast off too tightly so the work has some elasticity.

Casting off knitwise

1 Knit two stitches. Insert the point of the left-hand needle into the first stitch worked and pass it over the second stitch and off the right-hand needle.

2 One stitch is now on the right-hand needle. Knit the next stitch so there are two stitches on the right-hand needle and pass the first stitch over the second and off the needle as before. Repeat until there is just one stitch remaining. Break the yarn and draw through the last stitch to fasten off.

Casting off purlwise

To cast off in purl, repeat as for knitwise, working in purl stitch instead of knit.

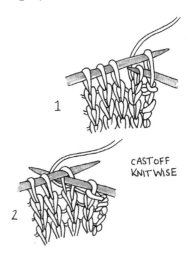

CASTOFF KNITWISE

INTARSIA

The intarsia technique uses blocks of colour to create a pattern. Small balls of yarn for each area of colour are twisted as they meet at the back of the work, rather than carrying them across the entire row, preventing tangling and keeping the stitches neat.

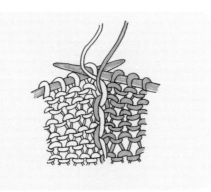

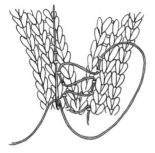
MATTRESS STITCH

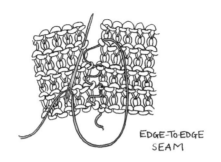
EDGE-TO-EDGE SEAM

Backstitch seam

It is important to make sure your stitches are neat and worked in a straight line. The backstitched seam gives a tailored finish to the work.

1 With right sides together and working one stitch in from the edge, begin by working a couple of stitches over each other to secure the seam.

2 Bring the needle through to the front of the work one stitch ahead of the last stitch made. Insert the needle back through the work at the end of the last stitch. Repeat step 2 to complete the seam.

SEAMS

Seams should be joined using a blunt-ended darning or tapestry needle and matching yarn, preferably a long length that has been left at the beginning or end of the work as it is already fastened in place. If you are joining in new yarn to sew the pieces together, leave a length at the beginning, which can be darned in afterwards to avoid any untidy ends showing. Make sure any patterns and shapings are matched.

Mattress stitch

Mattress stitch produces an invisible seam that is suitable for stocking-stitch fabric. It gives a lovely neat, straight finish. Place the two pieces side by side with right sides of work facing you. Insert the needle under the horizontal bar between the first two stitches on one side, then under the same bar on the other piece. Continue picking up the stitches and drawing the edges together, every few stitches, to join the seam.

Edge-to-edge seam

This is a suitable method for garter-stitch fabric and is also perfect for joining delicate articles as it creates a flat seam with elasticity. Place the two pieces of work together with the edges meeting and the right sides facing you. Join the seam by picking up a loop from the edge of each side alternately.

Slipstitch

Insert the needle into a stitch on the wrong side of the knitting and then into a stitch on the cast-on or cast-off edge. Repeat to the end, keeping the stitches even and not too tight.

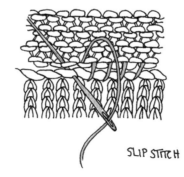
SLIP STITCH

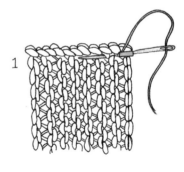
1

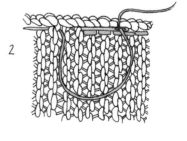
2

finishing touches

Pompoms and tassels are sewn to the ends of hat ties for decoration as well as added weight. Adding features with embroidery gives unique character to the animals.

TWISTED CORD

1 Measure the required number of strands and lengths of yarn and knot them together at the ends. Slip one end over a hook or doorknob and insert a pencil into the other end and hold between the thumb and forefinger, keeping the yarn taut. Turn the pencil clockwise to twist the strands.

2 Continue turning the pencil until the strands are tightly twisted. Fold them, allowing the two halves to twist together naturally. Remove the pencil and carefully undo the knots. With a strand threaded onto a needle, wind the yarn around the cord near the top and secure with a few stitches. Alternatively, the end can be knotted but will be bulkier.

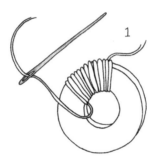

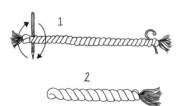

POMPOMS

1 Cut two circles of card to the required measurement for each pompom. Make a hole in the centre of each circle. The hole should be around a third of the size of the finished pompom. Thread a blunt needle with a long length of doubled yarn and, with the two circles of card together, wind the yarn through the hole and around the outer edge of the circle. Continue in this way, using new lengths of yarn until the hole is filled and the circle is covered.

2 Cut through the yarn around the outer edge between the two circles of card. Tie a length of yarn securely around the middle leaving long ends, which will be used to attach them to the cords. Remove the card and trim the pompom, fluffing it into shape.

TASSELS

1 Cut a piece of card to the required length of the finished tassel. Wind the yarn around the card to the desired thickness. Break yarn, leaving a long length, and thread it through a needle. Slip the needle through all the loops on the card and tie the yarn tightly at the top edge.

2 Remove the card and wind the yarn around the loops, a little way down from the tied top end, securing with a few stitches and drawing the needle through to the top to leave an end to stitch to the cord. Cut through the folded lower edge and trim to neaten the ends.

FRENCH KNOTS

1 Bring the yarn through to the right side of the work at the desired position the French knot is to be made and hold it down with the left thumb. Wind the yarn twice around the needle, still holding it firmly in place.

2 Insert the needle back into the work, close to the point where the yarn first appeared. Pull the yarn through to tighten the knot and then fasten off or bring the needle back through to the front of the work at the point where you wish to start another French knot.

EMBROIDERING WHISKERS

With the chosen shade of yarn threaded onto a blunt-ended needle, secure the end at the back of the work near to the nose.

1 Bring the needle through to the front at the point near the nose where you wish your whisker to start. Insert the needle into the work, through to the back at the point where you wish the whisker to end, making one long stitch.

2 Bring the needle through to the front at the point where you wish the second whisker to end. Insert the needle into the work, through to the back at the point where you wish the second whisker to begin, making one long stitch.

3 Repeat step 1 to complete the third whisker. Fasten off.

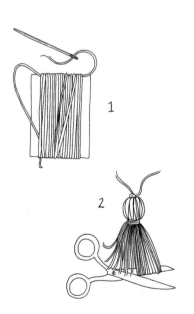

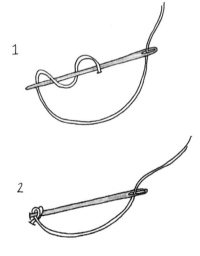

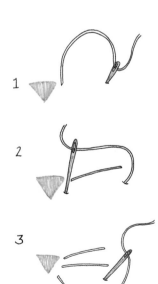

ABBREVIATIONS

alt	alternate	psso	pass slipped stitch
approx	approximately		over
beg	beginning	pfb	purl into front and
cm	centimetre(s)		back of next st
cont	continue	rem	remaining
dec	decrease	rep	repeat
DK	double knit	RH	right hand
foll	following	RS	right side
g-st	garter stitch	sl	slip
in	inch(es)	sl st	slip stitch
inc	increase by working	st(s)	stitch(es)
	into front and back of	st st	stocking stitch
	same stitch	tbl	through back of
K	knit		the loop
kfb	increase by working	tog	together
	into front and back	WS	wrong side
	of same stitch	yf	yarn forward
k2tog	decrease by knitting	*	work instructions
	two stitches together		immediately following
kwise	by knitting the st		*, then rep. as directed
meas	measures	( )	rep instructions
MC	main colour		inside brackets
ML	make loop		as many times as
P	purl		instructed
patt	pattern		
p2tog	purl 2 together		
p2togtbl	purl 2 together		
	through the		
	back loops		

CONVERSIONS

Knitting needle sizes

UK	Metric	US
14	2mm	0
13	2.5mm	1
12	2.75mm	2
11	3mm	–
10	3.25mm	3
–	3.5mm	4
9	3.75mm	5
8	4mm	6
7	4.5mm	7
6	5mm	8
5	5.5mm	9
4	6mm	10
3	6.5mm	10.5
2	7mm	10.5
1	7.5mm	11
0	8mm	11
00	9mm	13
000	10mm	15

UK/US yarn weights

UK	US
2-ply	Lace
3-ply	Fingering
4-ply	Sport
Double knitting (DK)	Light worsted
Aran	Fisherman/worsted
Chunky	Bulky
Super chunky	Extra bulky

SUPPLIERS

YARNS

Coats Crafts UK
Green Lane Mill
Holmfirth
West Yorkshire
HD9 2DX
Tel: +44 (0)1484 681881
Email: consumer.ccuk@coats.com
www.coatscrafts.co.uk

Deramores
Units 5–9 Tomas Seth Business Park
Argent Road
Queenborough
ME11 5TS
Tel: +44 (0)8455 194573
www.deramores.com

Designer Yarns Ltd
Unit 8-10 Newbridge Industrial
Estate,
Pitt Street, Keighley,
West Yorkshire BD21 4PQ
Tel : +44 (0)1535 664222
Email: david@designeryarns.uk.com
www.designeryarns.uk.com

Knitting Fever Inc.
315 Bayview Avenue
Amityville
New York
NY 11701
Tel: +1 516 546 3600
www.knittingfever.com

Plassard-Diffusion
La Filature
71800 Vareness-Sous-Dun
France
Tel: +33 (0)3 85 28 28 28
Email: info@plassard-diffusion.com
www.plassard-diffusion.com

Prestige Yarns Pty Ltd
PO Box 39
Bulli NSW 2516
Australia
Tel: + 61 (0)2 4285 6669
Email: info@prestigeyarns
www.prestigeyarns.com

Rowan (UK)
PO Box 22
Lingfield House
Lingfield Point
McMullen Road
Darlington
County Durham
DL1 1YQ
Tel: +44 (0)1484 681881
www.knitrowan.com

Sirdar Spinning Ltd
Flanshaw Lane
Wakefield
West Yorkshire WF2 9ND
Tel: +44 (0)1924 231 682
Email: consumer@sirdar.co.uk
www.sirdar.co.uk

Sublime
Tel: +44 (0) 1924 369666
Email: contactus@sublimeyarns.com
www.sublimeyarns.com

BUTTONS

MacCulloch and Wallis
25–26 Dering Street
London
W1S 1AT
Tel: +44 (0)20 7629 0311
Email: info@macculloch.com
www.macculloch-wallis.co.uk

Ray Stitch
99 Essex Road
London
N1 2SJ
Tel: +44 (0)20 7704 1060
Email: info@raystitch.co.uk
www.raystitch.co.uk

ABOUT THE AUTHOR

Vanessa Mooncie spent many happy hours as a child with her mother and grandmother, learning how to knit and crochet. She went on to study fashion and textile design and became a self-employed children's wear designer, illustrator and interior designer. She now specializes in silkscreen work and designing crochet jewellery through her company Kissy Suzuki (www.kissysuzuki. com). She lives with her family in a rural village in the south of England. Vanessa is also the author of Crocheted Accessories for GMC Publications and is a regular contributor to other craft books and magazines.

AUTHOR'S ACKNOWLEDGMENTS

Thank you to my family for their patience and support, especially Honey and Dolly – avid wearers of animal hats!

PUBLISHER'S ACKNOWLEDGMENTS

GMC Publications would like to thank the following people for their help in creating this book.

Main photography: Chris Gloag
Still life photography: Rebecca Mothersole
Model: Vanessa Grasse at Zone models
Hair and make-up: Jeni Dodson
Pattern checking: Jude Roust
Illustrations: Vanessa Mooncie

INDEX

To place an order, or to request a catalogue, contact:
GMC Publications, Castle Place, 166 High Street, Lewes, East Sussex, BN7 1XU United Kingdom
Tel: +44 (0)1273 488005
www.gmcbooks.com